Think, Read, Write

A Guide to Critical Thinking, Reading, and Writing

Kimberley Hardin

Texas A&M University Kingsville

Kendall Hunt

publishing company

Cover image © Singkham/Shutterstock.com

Kendall Hunt
publishing company

www.kendallhunt.com
Send all inquiries to:
4050 Westmark Drive
Dubuque, IA 52004-1840

Contents

Introduction

The significance of the title of this book lies in the ordering of the words: think, read, write. You can't do the last one without doing the first two. Using the cover picture as a metaphor, thinking is the soil, reading is the seed, and writing is the plant that grows from both of these things. You can also see critical thinking as the water that nourishes your writing; the more you think, the more you water your plant, the better your paper will be, and the bigger your plant will grow. This book teaches writing as a process that begins with thinking. But not just any thinking; there's thinking, and then there's *critical* thinking. A writer needs to be able to think and read critically before they produce their writing. That's why this book was created: to give students a foundation of critical thinking and reading skills that will nourish their writing skills, culminating in a successful thinker, a successful reader, and a successful writer.

In this book, we will learn what critical thinking is, as well as skills to improve our thinking. We then move on to reading critically and responding critically to texts. After that, we discuss the process of writing and rhetorical situations to consider when writing. Finally, we learn three different genres of writing, putting our newly formed critical thinking, reading, and writing skills into action. We will learn about conducting formal research, including how to find, evaluate, and incorporate sources into your writing. The last chapter in this book is a style guide to help you with grammar and punctuation.

By learning and practicing "the art of questioning," students build thinking, reading, and writing skills that will carry them throughout college and beyond. In summary, the purpose of this book is to promote the process of writing based on questioning and thinking, a writing guide that hopefully will empower students to become skilled thinkers and confident writers.

Chapter 1

Critical Thinking and Reading

"Education is not the learning of facts, but training the mind to think."

—**Albert Einstein**

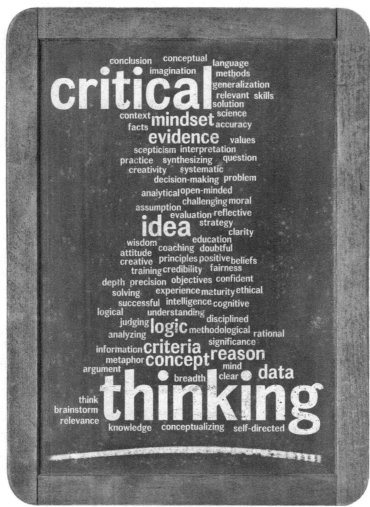

© marekuliasz/Shutterstock.com

> ## TEN-MINUTE PROMPT
>
> In your own words, define critical thinking. What is it, and how does one think critically? Do you ever examine your own thinking? If so, how?

What Is Critical Thinking?

What do you know about how to think? Have you ever analyzed your own thinking? Where do your opinions and beliefs come from? If you have never asked yourself these questions, then you're probably not a critical thinker. Most people aren't—because critical thinking isn't something that comes naturally; it's something you have to learn and practice, and unfortunately it's not a subject in most schools.

In order to understand critical thinking, we must first define it. The word *critical* literally means finding truth, merit, and judging for the same. When thinking critically, the brain is in a state of receiving information. Then the information is examined for merit. The word *critical* has several connotations also. Something is critical if an emergency situation is pushing a process, procedure, or action. People are called critical if they are judgmental. The root of the meaning comes from the activity of questioning and evaluating. The definition for critical thinking that fits in this case considers not the acts of being critical but rather the qualities of being critical: "Critical thinking qualities are a combination of cognitive abilities, basic attitudes, and thinking strategies that enable you to clarify and improve your understanding of the world" (Chaffee 71).

Some argue that we are all just products of our environments—that all of our opinions are shaped by our surroundings and influences. For instance, we have certain opinions and beliefs simply because we're Americans; we may have certain beliefs because we grew up poor, or rich, or in the country, or in the city. Children accept information from trusted sources many times without question, but through their experiences they learn more about discerning what information is faulty and what can be trusted. Often the trusted information is associated with a person who is an authority figure. Teachers, parents, and family members come under that category. As children grow older, they learn to verify information and they practice *becoming* the authority by sharing information they learn. Children can experience becoming an authority early in their lives as they learn from the Internet sources about animals, plants, and people, then share that knowledge with others. The experiences they gain through gaming can also become a place where they are in the seat of authority informing others. Life becomes more complicated and the sources that were once the authority on a topic become a limited source.

Our environments and experiences definitely have a hand in shaping us—but if we allow our surroundings to decide our beliefs for us, then our minds aren't really our own. So ask yourself: Where do my opinions come from? Do I believe something just because of my parents/upbringing/surroundings? Is my mind really my own?

Critical thinking doesn't mean simply being cynical. Being a critical thinker means being open-minded, reasonable, and rational. When you think critically, you go beyond your initial emotional reaction to think more deeply and analytically about the situation. Critical thinking means not taking something at face value, but looking beneath the surface to see what's really going on—what are this person's actual motives for saying or doing that? What are the likely causes or effects of this situation? It also means examining your own thinking, and accepting the possibility that you may be wrong.

A critical thinker:

- ▶ **Evaluates their own thinking:** This means thinking about why you think the way you think, where your opinions and beliefs come from, and how you can better your thinking.

- ▶ **Engages with the world around them:** What does it mean to be engaged with the world? It means paying attention and knowing what's going on around you; being informed about current news and events; engaging in open discussion with others; and taking part in the democratic process. It means being a part of the world, not just watching from the sidelines.

- ▶ **Values reason over emotion:** This is not to say that emotion is bad; we're humans, and emotion is a part of us. But at some point we have to go beyond our initial emotional reactions in order to think clearly. For example, after the Sandy Hook school shootings, everyone was in an emotional state, which was a proper response for such a tragedy. But many people used emotion to argue for or against gun control. Since gun violence is a very complex issue, we must be able to think rationally about it. A critical thinker sets aside emotions in order to think through an issue thoroughly and rationally.

- ▶ **Asks questions:** The most important thing a critical thinker does is question things. When implementing critical thinking skills, it seems that there is a list of never ending questions and that the more research there is, the more questions there are when seeking an answer. The decision-making process is complicated. One of the necessary passages in life include becoming a questioner. In college classes, it is rare that a student would look to a single source to come to a conclusion. Students are encouraged to question everything; question what you hear, what you think, what you say. Asking questions opens the mind to further avenues of thought.

Questions for Discussion

What point is the author making about colleges? About students? About faculty? Why is critical thinking important, according to the author?

The Art of Questioning

As we've said, asking questions is an important part of critical thinking. Thinking, reading, and writing all start with asking questions. Here are some important questions to ask when practicing critical thinking:

1. **What do I really think?** This is a serious and challenging question; serious because a critical thinker must be honest, and challenging because being honest is not always easy. Sometimes being honest means acknowledging that you don't have the answer, or that you don't know enough about a particular subject to truly have an informed opinion. This is also challenging because this is only the starting point; too often thinking stops with an opinion, but with critical thinking, we begin with an opinion, then question it.

2. **What does that word mean?** This goes beyond simply looking a word up in the dictionary; it also means questioning the implications of a word within a given sentence. The meaning of many words is open to question, as we'll learn in Chapter 4. Even words that seem commonplace need to be questioned. Often we don't question the meaning of words because we assume that *everyone* knows what they mean, but this assumption is usually wrong. Consider the words *cheating* and *enhancement*. *Enhancement* means anything people can do to improve their ability to perform; some students take drugs such as Adderall, a drug used to treat Attention Deficit Disorder, to help them study because it increases concentration and therefore enhances their ability to study. But if a student actually has ADD, taking the medication may not be considered enhancement, but only restoring the normal ability to concentrate. *Cheating* means violating the rules that all participants are supposed to observe. Can we call students' use of Adderall cheating? Only if the rules of their specific university prohibit the use of brain-enhancing drugs; otherwise, it's simply *enhancement*, not *cheating*.

3. **Is that statement accurate?** Just as we can fail to question the meaning of words because we assume everyone knows what they mean, so can we fail to examine the accuracy of statements because we assume everyone knows they are accurate. Consider the statement, "Adderall has no long-term side effects." How can we know if this statement is accurate? The answer is a matter of fact; to answer it, we'd have to locate authoritative information. Letting inaccurate statements slide by is another common way critical thinking goes wrong; it is just as common as not questioning the meaning of words.

4. **Is that statement true?** This is different from asking if a statement is accurate. Accuracy is a question of fact; truth is often a question of value. Consider the statement, "Peaceful co-existence is always a good thing." No amount of data can answer this question, because it is a question of belief and not accuracy. The answer to questions of belief must be based on our knowledge and experience. So, is

peaceful coexistence always a good thing? Is peaceful coexistence between slaves and their masters a good thing? What other conditions might also be intolerable?

5. **What does "x" assume?*** Almost every statement is based on assumptions. Asking questions can help us determine whether we should accept or challenge assumptions. For example, consider this statement: "Jane is smart; her IQ is 130." It assumes that the tests purporting to measure intelligence are reliable. Because the reliability of these tests is frequently disputed, we can challenge this assumption.

6. **What does "x" imply?** Asking questions about what follows from a statement can help us determine whether we should accept it. For example, if someone says, "Internet privacy should be protected no matter what," then you can ask, "Are you willing to give up free Internet access to protect your privacy?" "Are you willing to protect the privacy of terrorists?" You can ask these questions because the statement implies them.

7. **Is "x" a good analogy?** Frequently statements are based on analogies or comparisons. The claim that animals have rights, for example, is based on an analogy, a comparison with people's rights, such as the right to vote or the right to a trial by jury. Obviously animals do not have the same rights as human beings, so what rights should they have and why?

8. **How many kinds of "x" can we distinguish?** Often a single word or concept has many meanings. *Love* can mean the feelings of a parent for a child or a lover for the beloved. The biblical command to "love thy neighbor as thyself" has nothing to do with emotions. Here *love* means treating others with courtesy and respect. Many concepts are like "love"; they are used to refer to numerous situations or behaviors. We often need to distinguish among the meanings of a word.

9. **What is a good example of "x"?** Thinking of concrete examples can often help us understand and think critically about abstract ideas. For example, *peaceful coexistence* may initially seem a wonderful thing. However, when we think about a concrete example of peaceful coexistence, such as Britain and France peacefully coexisting with Nazi Germany in the 1930s, we realize that it may come at a high price.

10. **What are the likely consequences of "x"?** With any proposal for action, we should consider what is likely to happen. If someone says, "We should withdraw our troops from Afghanistan as soon as we can," we should ask questions like the following: "If we pull out, will Afghanistan again fall under Taliban control?" "Will the Taliban allow al-Qaeda to reestablish a base of operations there?" "What will happen to women and girls there?"

The art of questioning can help us critically examine any kind of text, from cartoons to academic books and articles. Use the ten questions on page 6 and 7 to examine the following news item. Bear in mind that you can question both what the writer said and anything said by others that the writer quotes.

*Source: From *Engaging Questions: A Guide to Writing* by Carolyn Channell and Timothy Crusius. Copyright © 2013 by The McGraw-Hill Companies, Inc. Reprinted by permission.

Study: Students Need More Paths to Career Success

Christine Armario (Associated Press)

The current U.S. education system is failing to prepare millions of young adults for successful careers by providing a one-size-fits-all approach, and it should take a cue from its European counterparts by offering greater emphasis on occupational instruction, a Harvard University study published Wednesday concludes.

The two-year study by the Pathways to Prosperity Project at the Harvard University Graduate School of Education notes that while much emphasis is placed in high school on going on to a four-year college, only 30 percent of young adults in the United States successfully complete a bachelor's degree.

While the number of jobs that require no post-secondary education has declined, the researchers note that only one-third of the jobs created in the coming years are expected to need a bachelor's degree or higher. Roughly the same amount will need just an associate's degree or an occupational credential.

"What I fear is the continuing problem of too many kids dropping by the wayside and the other problem of kids going into debt, and going into college but not completing with a degree or certificate," said Robert Schwartz, who heads the project and is academic dean of the Harvard Graduate School of Education. "Almost everybody can cite some kid who marched off to college because it was the only socially legitimate thing to do but had no real interest!"

The report highlights an issue that has been percolating among education circles: That school reform should include more emphasis on career-driven alternatives to a four-year education.

The study recommends a "comprehensive pathways network" that would include three elements: embracing multiple approaches to help youth make the transition to adulthood, involving the nation's employers in things like work-based learning, and creating a new social compact with young people.

Many of the ideas aren't new, and leaders, including President Barack Obama, have advocated an increased role for community colleges so the country can once again lead the world in the proportion of college graduates.

U.S. Education Secretary Arne Duncan delivered opening remarks at the report's release in Washington on Wednesday, saying career and technical education has been "the neglected stepchild of education reform!"

"That neglect has to stop," Duncan said.

But the idea of providing more alternatives, rather than emphasizing a four-year college education for all, hasn't been without controversy. Critics fear students who opt early for a vocational approach might limit their options later on, or that disadvantaged students at failing schools would be pushed into technical careers and away from the highly selective colleges where their numbers are already very slim.

"Nobody who spends much time in America's high schools could possibly argue that they are focused on college for all, or ever have been," said Kati Haycock, president of The Education Trust, a nonpartisan Washington, D.C.-based think tank. "Most schools still resist that idea, instead continuing long-standing, unfair practices of sorting and selecting like an educational caste system—directing countless young people, especially low-income students and students of color, away from college-prep courses and from seeing themselves as "college material."

Schwartz said efforts should be intensified to get more low-income and minority students into selective institutions, while also strengthening the capacity of two-year colleges.

"You've got to work on both fronts at once," Schwartz said.

The study recommends that all major occupations be clearly outlined at the start of high school. Students would see directly how their course choices prepare them for careers that interest them—but still be able to change their minds. Students should also be given more opportunities for work-based learning, such as job shadowing and internships.

Students, the researchers recommend, should get career counseling and work-related opportunities early on—no later than middle school. In high school, students would have access to educational programs designed with the help of industry leaders, and they'd be able to participate in paid internships.

The report notes that many European countries already have such an approach, and that their youth tend to have a smoother transition into adulthood. And not all separate children into different paths at an early age. Finland and Denmark, for example, provide all students with a comprehensive education through grades 9 or 10. Then they are allowed to decide what type of secondary education they'd like to pursue.

Barney Bishop, president and CEO of Associated Industries of Florida, said he would advocate an approach that provides more alternatives and greater inclusion of the business community.

"The problem for the business community is where you have kids who don't have the rudimentary skills, and you have to take the time and effort to train them, get them some of the rudimentary skills, plus the special skills," he said.

Sandy Baum, an independent higher education policy analyst, said she thinks there needs to be more counseling in advising students about how to make the right choices. "I don't think the problem is too many people going to four-year colleges," she said. "The problem is too many people making inappropriate choices."

"What we'd like is a system where people of all backgrounds could choose to be plumbers or to be philosophers," Baum added. "Those options are not open. But we certainly need plumbers, so it's wrong to think we should be nervous about directing people in that route!"

This chart shows the process of critical thinking. As you can see, all the stages are ongoing, suggesting that critical thinking is a cyclical pattern of thinking.

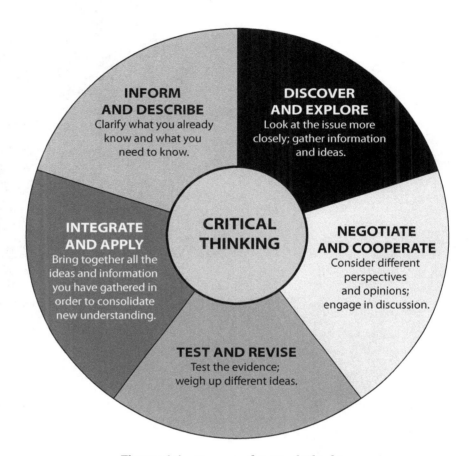

Figure 1.1   Process of Critical Thinking

What Is Critical Reading?

Critical reading is basically reading with questions—*what* is this author saying? *How* is (s)he saying it–does (s)he use humor? Symbolism? An appeal to emotions? *Why* is (s)he saying it? And, most importantly, *do I agree with what the author is saying?* Why or why not?

Critical thinking is an essential skill—and writing (and reading) are vital to learning it. Writing is nothing if not *a process of critical inquiry.*

Critical reading and writing means reading and writing with questions. Critical reading requires you to actively engage with the text—this is different from how we typically read, which is just to complete the reading for the assignment. When we do this kind of reading, we've wasted our time—we haven't engaged with the text, we haven't read critically, so we haven't learned anything.

© Minerva Studio/Shutterstock.com

Here are some reading strategies to help you interact with the text and build your critical thinking skills:

Before reading

- ► Establish your purpose.
  - ▪ Why are you reading? To learn? To be entertained? To be persuaded?
  - ▪ What do you hope to gain by reading this?
  - ▪ Set a purpose and goals beforehand so you know why you're reading and what you want to get from it.
- ► Preview the text:
  - ▪ Read the title and back cover.
  - ▪ Read the table of contents.
  - ▪ Read the author's information.
  - ▪ Become familiar with the book and the author.
- ► Make predictions and access background knowledge:
  - ▪ What do you think the text will be about?
  - ▪ What do you already know about this subject?

During reading

- ► Ask questions
  - ▪ What is the author's purpose—to inform, entertain, or persuade?
  - ▪ What is the author's intended audience?
  - ▪ What is the author saying about the subject?
  - ▪ What assumptions is the author making? Does the author bring any biases to the text?

- How does the author get his/her point across to the audience? Does he/she use humor? Anecdotes? Appeals to the emotions?
- Do you agree with what the author is saying? Why or why not?
- Are there any words or phrases that are unfamiliar? Look them up in the glossary or a dictionary.
  ► Engage with the text:
- Don't be passive—think about what you are reading.
- Write any questions or comments in the margins.
- Use what you already know about the subject to form your own opinions.

After reading

► Summarize what you've read.
► Read over your notes.
► Challenge your own reactions.
► Identify the key concepts or the main idea.
► Summarize or sequence the events.
► Point out details or describe significant parts.
► Ask specific questions.
► Make connections (to self, text, and world).
► Compare/contrast/analyze.
► Make inferences.
► State opinions/point of view.
► Draw conclusions.
► Share insights and understandings.

Asking the Right Questions While Reading

Ask This	What Is Your Response?
Why am I reading this?	Purpose
What is the text structure? Genre? What visual information is in the chapter? (Tables, charts, pictures, etc.) What information is bolded?	Previewing
What are the main ideas and supporting details?	Skimming
What do I know about the topic from my prior learning and from my experiences?	Background
Can I use a graphic structure for the reading?	Graphic Organizer
Read the text with a varied speed, slowing for the new information and skimming if the information is known. Stop and make notes, re-read if you do not comprehend the text.	Make marginal notes through paraphrasing or summarizing, highlight key vocabulary.
Make connections between the reading and what you know about the topic either from lecture or past experiences. Note any conflicts and write a question that you can ask in class.	Formulate clarifying questions for class.
Note the information that is being learned.	Use a bulleted list or short notes to record information.
Organize the information into a visual learning tool.	Reflect and connect

Analyzing Discourse Community Journal Articles

A discourse community has six distinct characteristics (Swales, 2014). When evaluating the material the questions to ask are critical to formulating informed personal conclusions (Gee, 2014). Read with a questioning attitude. Interact and evaluate arguments using knowledge and dependable opinions. Question as you read to acquire new knowledge through questions designed to uncover decisions or beliefs.

What did the researcher want to know?	When trying to find an answer, what did the researcher learn?
What population did the researcher decide to use?	Which method did the researcher set up?
What type of data did the researcher create?	What did the researcher find out?
What implications is the result of the research?	What limitations does the research have?
Why is the author making various claims?	What is the intent of the journal article?
Are there conflicts within the community? If so, why?	Do some participants have difficulties? Why?
Who has authority? Where does the authority come from?	What are the modes of belonging to the discourse community that the newcomers use?
What sorts of multi-literacies do members possess?	Are members stereotyped in any way in regard to literacy knowledge?
What questions does the text address either explicitly or implicitly?	Why does the author or the community care about the issues in the article?
Who is the intended audience? Are you part of the audience?	How does the author support the thesis with reasons/evidence?
Are the arguments convincing? Why?	Was the counter argument addressed?
How does the author interest the reader?	Do the appeals used by the author work for the reader or make the reader suspicious of the author's motives?
How does the author obtain credibility with the audience?	Is the author credible to the reader?
Are the author's sources reliable?	Are the writer's basic beliefs, values, and assumptions similar to or different from the reader? How does the writer's world view coincide with my own?
How do I respond to this text?	Will the reader go along with or challenge the text presented?
How has the article changed the reader's thinking?	How well does this author's evident purposes for writing fit with what the reader learned from the text?

Of course, reading critically means you have to challenge your own opinions as well. So go beyond your initial reaction to the text and analyze yourself—why did I have this reaction? What experience/knowledge do I have about this subject that may affect my opinion? What assumptions/biases am I bringing to this text? Do I know enough about this topic to have an informed opinion?

One of the most flexible strategies for college reading is **annotation**. Annotations are notes in the margins that allow you to comment on and ask questions about the text you're reading. The strategy of reading with a pencil or pen in hand helps the reading make sense as the paragraphs are read. Most reading comprehension coaches talk about using a pencil to annotate text while reading, because the act of writing while reading is beneficial for both visual and active learners. The annotation strategy works with the brain on many levels, but the one the brain likes best is that the strategy is flexible and individual. The flexibility of annotation helps the reader interact with the text in a way that helps the reader. What is important about the strategy is that when you are reading with a pencil in hand you are actively engaged. It is difficult to fall asleep when writing in the text. Reading a text as you are annotating will help you remember what you read, help you find information that you read (making re-reading the entire text unnecessary), and help you connect with the author's information on deeper levels.

Here are some questions your annotations might answer:

▶ **What words do I not know?** If you come across an unfamiliar word, it's important that you either look the word up in a dictionary or use **context clues** to help you figure out the meaning. Why is this important? The more words you skip, the less you comprehend. Looking up unfamiliar words will help build your vocabulary and enable you to **infer** the meaning of words in the future, which will allow you more time to engage with the ideas presented in the text.

> What are context clues, and how does one infer? Inferences are educated guesses about what we do not know, based on what we do know. Context clues are clues within the sentence that help us find the meaning of a word. Consider the following selection:
>
> > For me, as for others, the Net is becoming a universal medium, a conduit for most of the information that <u>flows</u> through my eyes and ears and into my mind . . . As the media theorist Marshall McLuhan pointed out in the 1960's, media are not just passive <u>channels</u> of information.
> >
> > Nicholas Carr, "Is Google Making Us Stupid?," *The Atlantic,* July/August 2008 issue.
>
> If the word conduit is unfamiliar, you can use the surrounding words to infer its meaning. Based on the other words in the passage, what do you think a conduit is?

▶ **What are the main points of the passage?** Mark the main ideas in the margins so you can easily find them later. This will help you comprehend the text even further and allow you to easily look back and remind yourself what you read.

▶ **What words signal the author's train of thought?** Words such as "however" and "but" show that the author will contradict something just stated. Expressions like "for example" suggest that the author will elaborate on an idea. Circle or underline these words, and note how the author's train of thought shifts.

▶ **Where does the author introduce viewpoints other than his or her own?** Take note of when an author introduces people who agree or disagree with their ideas, and how they respond to those counterarguments.

▶ **How well am I comprehending this reading?** If you find some parts of a text difficult to comprehend, put a question mark in the margin to tell yourself what you need to return to later. If you can connect any prior knowledge, observation, or personal opinion to something in the text, note it in the margin.

Some of the beneficial marks in text can be simple indicators of the reader's attitude of the content of the text, i.e., "√" for I agree, "X" for I don't agree, and "?" for what does this mean? Readers can use personal markings that are only meaningful to them also. It really doesn't matter that much. That is the beauty of this particular strategy; freedom to mark to make sense on your own terms! Some readers make comments as they read such as, "That's what the professor said" or "That is different from what the professor said." The whole reason we annotate is to keep from re-reading the entire text. Side annotations create markers for the concepts in text, so when studying for a test, it is easy to slide down the side markers to find information for the study guides. Commentary on the side makes looking back to the textbook easier.

Here is a chart that breaks down another way you might annotate a text:

Step	Why do?
1. Number the paragraphs	Numbering the paragraphs helps when back in class. If the professor is leading a discussion, it is easy to scan back down the left hand margin to notes made while reading. So numbering the paragraphs keep you from scouring the book to see what everyone is talking about.
2. Chunk the text	Text structure provides readers with natural starts and stops in reading. When reading, it is helpful to pay attention to the breaks, to provide a marker of when to stop and start writing. Paragraphs made be the perfect marker when reading a literary text, but when reading a content text, the markers are bolded subtitles! So group the text in chunks for reading!
3. Underline and circle… with a purpose	Using the underlining and circle calls attention to text. Use the marks with a purpose. Circle unknown vocabulary, underline sentences that tell the main idea. Using underlines and circles are a great way to call attention to facts in the text or information that relates to the lecture from class. Use them judicially, purposefully. They will quickly become marks that are personal.
Vocabulary	When marking key vocabulary, the words are usually content related vocabulary and are defined in the text. These key words are related closely to the content (discourse community) being covered in the text. They are also vocabulary words that will be used in the classroom, so they are very important to know and use. Key terms in the text are words that: 1. Are defined. 2. Are repeated throughout the text. 3. Hold meaning for the content, meaning knowing the vocabulary will sum up the content just covered!

4. Left margin: What is the author SAYING?	The left margin is a great place to make sense of the reading. The reader uses the space to paraphrase, summarize, or call out facts that are necessary for understanding the content. Some readers use markings for the side margins. I don't agree. ✗ I agree. ✚ This doesn't add up. ≠ Question for class. ? **Professors love these! Ask them to answer them while you are in class.** The individual reader decides what to use. As long as there is some active thinking about the content being read, the reader is likely to remember the text.
5. Right margin: Dig deeper into the text	In Nancy Wood's book, *College Reading and Study Skills*, the right hand margin is a place to begin deeper comprehension. The deeper comprehension is all about critically reacting to the text. Represent the text in a picture. Ask a question. The main focus of this side note is that the reader is beginning to connect the content to the context of the world. Making connections to the content by relating it to the world around simply means that the reader is relating it to their personal lives, the world around them, or to other content in their background. Making those types of connections are part of using the new information to build on what is already in the memory.

Paraphrasing Difficult Passages*

The reading you do in college is sometimes difficult. Paraphrasing can help you make sense of challenging passages. A paraphrase is a *restatement in your own words and sentences*. Paraphrasing is like translating the passage into language you can better understand—using shorter, more direct sentences and more familiar vocabulary. It ought to substitute your own language for the author's voice, sentence patterns, and word choices. A paraphrase should be in your own voice, which usually means trading more literal language for any metaphors or similes, unless you put them in quotation marks.

The following is a passage from Codrescu's reading in which he explains the immigrant's disillusionment with American material goods. Note that the paraphrase, on the right, is approximately as long as the original. A paraphrase is not a summary, and it should contain all of the points in the original passage. As the color coding indicates, all the points in the original appear in the paraphrase.

*From *Engaging Questions: A Guide to Writing* by Carolyn Channell and Timothy Crusius. Copyright © 2013 by The McGraw-Hill Companies, Inc. Reprinted by permission.

Original Passage	**Paraphrase**
When you first arrive on these shores, you are in mourning. The only consolations are these products, which had been imbued with religious significance back at home. But when these things turn out not to be the real things, you begin to experience a second death, brought about by betrayal. You begin to suspect that the religious significance you had attached to them was only possible back home, where these things did not exist. Here, where they are plentiful, they have no significance whatsoever. They are inanimate fetishes, somebody else's fetishes, no help to you at all.	New immigrants to America feel the loss of their friends, family, and culture. Codrescu compares this sense of loss to mourning a death. To console themselves, they turn to material objects such as cars and furniture, things that they could not buy in the old country but could only dream of possessing. They believed in the power of these objects to give meaning to life. But the immigrant discovers, sadly, that the products are cheap and shoddily made. This discovery is a second loss, as the immigrant mourns the loss of hope. Paradoxically, the products had meaning only in the old country, when they were out of reach. Here, they are nothing but junk, and the buyer finds that they are useless in providing any sort of consolation.

Summarizing the Text

Writing a summary of a reading helps you see the text as a whole, not a series of parts. It is often necessary to sum up the entire content of a reading, such as when you want to explain someone else's argument in a paper of your own or when writing an annotated bibliography to let others know the content of your sources.

To write a summary, you must first sort out the main ideas from the supporting details and then put the main ideas into your own words—that is, paraphrase them. Writing a descriptive outline, as explained above, is an excellent strategy for drafting a summary. Once you have found the major subdivisions of a reading and paraphrased their key points, you have material to work with for a summary.

Simply splicing the paraphrases together, however, may not result in a smooth summary. The biggest challenge is to unite these paraphrases into a coherent piece of writing that reflects the train of thought in the original passage. You will need to add transitions and possibly some additional information from the original text. You may use brief quotations. Bear in mind, however, that a summary should be no more than one-third the length of the original.

Responding to a Reading

During and after rereading, you should have more extensive responses to a stimulating text, with more thoughts than can fit in a marginal note. That is why serious readers and researchers keep reading response journals for recording thoughts, reactions, and opinions that are more extensive than brief annotations.

You could simply write your thoughts in a spiral notebook or in a file you keep on your computer, or you could follow the suggestion of many reading experts and use a double-entry journal, a notebook, or online document divided into two columns with quotations or paraphrases of the text in one column and your reactions on the right. Following is an example of a double-entry reading journal:

What the text says:	What I say back to the text:
Par. 2: Codrescu shows how isolated immigrants can be: "there was no one with whom to make toasts and sing songs."	This passage explains why many new immigrants want to live in neighborhoods with others who share their customs and language. I think as they assimilate, they lose this dependency, but that is sad too because their children often forget about their roots.
Par. 3: "She had traded in her friends and relatives for ersatz tomatoes, fake chicken, phony furniture."	His mother expected American products to be a good part, and they weren't. Why not? Possibly because Americans are more interested in saving money on necessities like food and furniture so they can spend it on other more status-symbol things.
Par. 4: "She deplored its rudeness, its insensitivity, its outright meanness, its indifference, the chase after the almighty buck, the social isolation of most Americans, their inability to partake in warm, genuine fellowship and, above all, their deplorable lack of awe before what they had made."	This is a pretty harsh description of Americans. It shows how an outsider notices the downside of our fast-paced, materialistic lifestyle—things that we might acknowledge if pointed out to us, but that we just accept as how it is. It would be interesting to get other opinions about this, such as from exchange students.

What the text says:	What I say back to the text:
Par. 6: ". . . she had left behind a vast range of daily humiliations."	Romania has changed now that it is a democracy and part of the European Union. She may not even want to leave if she lived there today, but the point of the essay is still relevant because it describes a universal experience for the many who still want to escape to America for freedom and a better life.
Par. 8: "America is a place of paradoxes. . . ."	What does he mean here? What other examples can I think of? An example would be American middle-class women who can choose to eat a healthy diet but are forced by fashion images to eat the calorie intake of someone in a developing country. They are free and yet they are controlled by media messages. That's a paradox.

The advantage of the double-entry journal is that it shows the connection between what you read and what you thought about what you read. The double-entry journal is useful for stimulating your own thinking in response to the text. You can also consult it for citing the passages in the text when writing in response to a reading.

Becoming a Critic of Your Thinking*

by Dr. Linda Elder and Dr. Richard Paul

Learning the Art of Critical Thinking

There is nothing more practical than sound thinking. No matter what your circumstance or goals, no matter where you are, or what problems you face, you are better off if your thinking is skilled. As a manager, leader, employee, citizen, lover, friend, parent—in every realm and situation of your life—good thinking pays off. Poor thinking, in turn, inevitably causes problems, wastes time and energy, engenders frustration and pain.

"Learning the Art of Critical Thinking" by Dr. Linda Elder and Dr. Richard Paul from the Foundation for Critical Thinking. © Foundation for Critical Thinking, www.criticalthinking.org. Reprinted by permission.

Critical thinking is the disciplined art of ensuring that you use the best thinking you are capable of in any set of circumstances. The general goal of thinking is to "figure out the lay of the land" in any situation we are in. We all have multiple choices to make. We need the best information to make the best choices.

What is really going on in this or that situation? Are they trying to take advantage of me? Does so-and-so really care about me? Am I deceiving myself when I believe that . . .? What are the likely consequences of failing to . . .? If I want to do . . . , what is the best way to prepare for it? How can I be more successful in doing . . .? Is this my biggest problem, or do I need to focus my attention on something else?

Successfully responding to such questions is the daily work of thinking. However, to maximize the quality of your thinking, you must learn how to become an effective "critic" of your thinking. And to become an effective critic of your thinking, you have to make learning about thinking a priority.

Ask yourself these—rather unusual—questions: What have you learned about how you think? Did you ever study your thinking? What do you know about how the mind processes information? What do you really know about how to analyze, evaluate, or reconstruct your thinking? Where does your thinking come from? How much of it is of "good" quality? How much of it is of "poor" quality? How much of your thinking is vague, muddled, inconsistent, inaccurate, illogical, or superficial? Are you, in any real sense, in control of your thinking? Do you know how to test it? Do you have any conscious standards for determining when you are thinking well and when you are thinking poorly? Have you ever discovered a significant problem in your thinking and then changed it by a conscious act of will? If anyone asked you to teach them what you have learned, thus far in your life, about thinking, would you really have any idea what that was or how you learned it?

If you are like most, the only honest answers to these questions run along the lines of, "Well, I suppose I really don't know much about my thinking or about thinking in general. I suppose in my life I have more or less taken my thinking for granted. I don't really know how it works. I have never really studied it. I don't know how I test it, or even if I do test it. It just happens in my mind automatically."

It is important to realize that serious study of thinking, serious thinking about thinking, is rare. It is not a subject in most colleges. It is seldom found in the thinking of our culture. But if you focus your attention for a moment on the role that thinking is playing in your life, you may come to recognize that, in fact, everything you do, or want, or feel is influenced by your thinking. And if you become persuaded of that, you will be surprised that humans show so little interest in thinking.

To make significant gains in the quality of your thinking you will have to engage in a kind of work that most humans find unpleasant, if not painful — intellectual work. Yet once this thinking is done and we move our thinking to a higher level of quality, it is not hard to keep it at that level. Still, there is the price you have to pay to step up to the next level. One doesn't become a skillful critic of thinking over night, any more than one becomes a skillful basketball player or musician over night. To become better at thinking, you must be willing to put the work into thinking that skilled improvement always requires.

This means you must be willing to practice special "acts" of thinking that are initially at least uncomfortable, and sometimes challenging and difficult. You have to learn to do with your mind "moves" analogous to what accomplished athletes learn to do (through practice and feedback) with their bodies. Improvement in thinking, in other words, is similar to improvement in other domains of performance where progress is a product of sound theory, commitment, hard work, and practice.

Consider the following key ideas, which, when applied, result in a mind practicing skilled thinking. These ideas represent just a few of the many ways in which disciplined thinkers actively apply theory of mind to the mind by the mind in order to think better. In these examples, we focus on the significance of thinking clearly, sticking to the point (thinking with relevance), questioning deeply, and striving to be more reasonable. For each example, we provide a brief overview of the idea and its importance in thinking, along with strategies for applying it in life. Realize that the following ideas are immersed in a cluster of ideas within critical thinking. Though we chose these particular ideas, many others could have instead been chosen. There is no magic in these specific ideas. In short, it is important that you understand these as a sampling of all the possible ways in which the mind can work to discipline itself, to think at a higher level of quality, to function better in the world.

1. Clarify Your Thinking

Be on the look-out for vague, fuzzy, formless, blurred thinking. Try to figure out the real meaning of what people are saying. Look on the surface. Look beneath the surface. Try to figure out the real meaning of important news stories. Explain your understanding of an issue to someone else to help clarify it in your own mind. Practice summarizing in your own words what others say. Then ask them if you understood them correctly. You should neither agree nor disagree with what anyone says until you (clearly) understand them.

Our own thinking usually seems clear to us, even when it is not. But vague, ambiguous, muddled, deceptive, or misleading thinking are significant problems in human life. If we are to develop as thinkers, we must learn the art of clarifying thinking, of pinning it down, spelling it out, and giving it a specific meaning. Here's what you can do to begin. When people explain things to you, summarize in your own words what you think they said. When you cannot do this to their satisfaction, you don't really understand what they said. When they cannot summarize what you have said to your satisfaction, they don't really understand what you said. Try it. See what happens.

Strategies for Clarifying Your Thinking

- ► State one point at a time
- ► Elaborate on what you mean
- ► Give examples that connect your thoughts to life experiences

► Use analogies and metaphors to help people connect your ideas to a variety of things they already understand (for example, critical thinking is like an onion. There are many layers to it. Just when you think you have it basically figured out, you realize there is another layer, and then another, and another and another and on and on)

Here Is One Format You Can Use

► I think . . . (state your main point)
► In other words . . . (elaborate your main point)
► For example . . . (give an example of your main point)
► To give you an analogy . . . (give an illustration of your main point)

To Clarify Other People's Thinking, Consider Asking the Following

► Can you restate your point in other words? I didn't understand you.
► Can you give an example?
► Let me tell you what I understand you to be saying. Did I understand you correctly?

2. Stick to the Point

Be on the look out for fragmented thinking, thinking that leaps about with no logical connections. Start noticing when you or others fail to stay focused on what is relevant. Focus on finding what will aid you in truly solving a problem. When someone brings up a point (however true) that doesn't seem pertinent to the issue at hand, ask, "How is what you are saying relevant to the issue?" When you are working through a problem, make sure you stay focused on what sheds light on and, thus, helps address the problem. Don't allow your mind to wander to unrelated matters. Don't allow others to stray from the main issue. Frequently ask: "What is the central question? Is this or that relevant to it? How?"

When thinking is relevant, it is focused on the main task at hand. It selects what is germane, pertinent, and related. It is on the alert for everything that connects to the issue. It sets aside what is immaterial, inappropriate, extraneous, and beside the point. What is relevant directly bears upon (helps solve) the problem you are trying to solve. When thinking drifts away from what is relevant, it needs to be brought back to what truly makes a difference. Undisciplined thinking is often guided by associations (this reminds me of that, that reminds me of this other thing) rather than what is logically connected ("If a and b are true, then c must also be true"). Disciplined thinking intervenes when thoughts wander from what is pertinent and germane concentrating the mind on only those things that help it figure out what it needs to figure out.

Ask These Questions to Make Sure Thinking Is Focused on What Is Relevant

► Am I focused on the main problem or task?
► How is this connected? How is that?
► Does my information directly relate to the problem or task?

> ► Where do I need to focus my attention?
> ► Are we being diverted to unrelated matters?
> ► Am I failing to consider relevant viewpoints?
> ► How is your point relevant to the issue we are addressing?
> ► What facts are actually going to help us answer the question? What considerations should be set aside?
> ► Does this truly bear on the question? How does it connect?

3. Question Questions

Be on the look out for questions. The ones we ask. The ones we fail to ask. Look on the surface. Look beneath the surface. Listen to how people question, when they question, when they fail to question. Look closely at the questions asked. What questions do you ask, should you ask? Examine the extent to which you are a questioner, or simply one who accepts the definitions of situations given by others.

Most people are not skilled questioners. Most accept the world as it is presented to them. And when they do question, their questions are often superficial or "loaded." Their questions do not help them solve their problems or make better decisions. Good thinkers routinely ask questions in order to understand and effectively deal with the world around them. They question the status quo. They know that things are often different from the way they are presented. Their questions penetrate images, masks, fronts, and propaganda. Their questions make real problems explicit and discipline their thinking through those problems. If you become a student of questions, you can learn to ask powerful questions that lead to a deeper and more fulfilling life. Your questions become more basic, essential, and deep.

Strategies for Formulating More Powerful Questions

> ► Whenever you don't understand something, ask a question of clarification.
> ► Whenever you are dealing with a complex problem, formulate the question you are trying to answer in several different ways (being as precise as you can) until you hit upon the way that best addresses the problem at hand.
> ► Whenever you plan to discuss an important issue or problem, write out in advance the most significant questions you think need to be addressed in the discussion. Be ready to change the main question, but once made clear, help those in the discussion stick to the question, making sure the dialogue builds toward an answer that makes sense.

Questions You Can Ask to Discipline Your Thinking

> ► What precise question are we trying to answer?
> ► Is that the best question to ask in this situation?
> ► Is there a more important question we should be addressing?
> ► Does this question capture the real issue we are facing?
> ► Is there a question we should answer before we attempt to answer this question?

> ▶ What information do we need to answer the question?
> ▶ What conclusions seem justified in light of the facts?
> ▶ What is our point of view? Do we need to consider another?
> ▶ Is there another way to look at the question?
> ▶ What are some related questions we need to consider?
> ▶ What type of question is this: an economic question, a political question, a legal question, etc.?

4. Be Reasonable

Be on the lookout for reasonable and unreasonable behaviors—yours and others. Look on the surface. Look beneath the surface. Listen to what people say. Look closely at what they do. Notice when you are unwilling to listen to the views of others, when you simply see yourself as right and others as wrong. Ask yourself at those moments whether their views might have any merit. See if you can break through your defensiveness to hear what they are saying. Notice unreasonableness in others. Identify times when people use language that makes them appear reasonable, though their behavior proves them to be otherwise. Try to figure out why you, or others, are being unreasonable. Might you have a vested interested in not being open-minded? Might they?

One of the hallmarks of a critical thinker is the disposition to change one's mind when given good reason to change. Good thinkers want to change their thinking when they discover better thinking. They can be moved by reason. Yet, comparatively few people are reasonable. Few are willing to change their minds once set. Few are willing to suspend their beliefs to fully hear the views of those with which they disagree. How would you rate yourself?

Strategies for Becoming More Reasonable

Say aloud, "I'm not perfect. I make mistakes. I'm often wrong." See if you have the courage to admit this during a disagreement: "Of course, I may be wrong. You may be right."

Practice saying in your own mind, "I may be wrong. I often am. I'm willing to change my mind when given good reasons." Then look for opportunities to make changes in your thinking.

Ask yourself, "When was the last time I changed my mind because someone gave me better reasons for his (her) views than I had for mine?" (To what extent are you open to new ways of looking at things? To what extent can you objectively judge information that refutes what you already think?)

Realize That You Are Being Close-Minded If You

1. are unwilling to listen to someone's reasons

2. are irritated by the reasons people give you

3. become defensive during a discussion

After you catch yourself being close-minded, analyze what was going on in your mind by completing these statements:

1. I realize I was being close-minded in this situation because . . .

2. The thinking I was trying to hold onto is . . .

3. Thinking that is potentially better is . . .

4. This thinking is better because . . .

In closing, let me remind you that the ideas in this article are a very few of the many ways in which critical thinkers bring intellectual discipline to bear upon their thinking. The best thinkers are those who understand the development of thinking as a process occurring throughout many years of practice in thinking. They recognize the importance of learning about the mind, about thoughts, feelings and desires and how these functions of the mind interrelate. They are adept at taking thinking apart, and then assessing the parts when analyzed. In short, they study the mind, and they apply what they learn about the mind to their own thinking in their own lives.

The extent to which any of us develops as a thinker is directly determined by the amount of time we dedicate to our development, the quality of the intellectual practice we engage in, and the depth, or lack thereof, of our commitment to becoming more reasonable, rational, successful persons.

Thinking Gets Us into Trouble Because We Often:

- ► jump to conclusions
- ► fail to think-through implications
- ► lose track of their goal
- ► are unrealistic
- ► focus on the trivial
- ► fail to notice contradictions
- ► accept inaccurate information
- ► ask vague questions
- ► give vague answers
- ► ask loaded questions
- ► ask irrelevant questions
- ► confuse questions of different types
- ► answer questions we are not competent to answer
- ► come to conclusions based on inaccurate or irrelevant information

- ► ignore information that does not support our view
- ► make inferences not justified by our experience
- ► distort data and state it inaccurately
- ► fail to notice the inferences we make
- ► come to unreasonable conclusions
- ► fail to notice our assumptions
- ► often make unjustified assumptions
- ► miss key ideas
- ► use irrelevant ideas
- ► form confused ideas
- ► form superficial concepts
- ► misuse words
- ► ignore relevant viewpoints
- ► cannot see issues from points of view other than our own
- ► confuse issues of different types
- ► are unaware of our prejudices
- ► think narrowly
- ► think imprecisely
- ► think illogically
- ► think one-sidedly
- ► think simplistically
- ► think hypocritically
- ► think superficially
- ► think ethnocentrically
- ► think egocentrically
- ► think irrationally
- ► do poor problem solving
- ► make poor decisions
- ► are poor communicators
- ► have little insight into our own ignorance

A How-To List for Dysfunctional Living

Most people have no notion of what it means to take charge of their lives. They don't realize that the quality of their lives depends on the quality of their thinking. We all engage in numerous dysfunctional practices to avoid facing problems in our thinking. Consider the following and ask yourself how many of these dysfunctional ways of thinking you engage in:

1. Surround yourself with people who think like you. Then no one will criticize you.

2. Don't question your relationships. You then can avoid dealing with problems within them.

3. If critiqued by a friend or lover, look sad and dejected and say, "I thought you were my friend!" or "I thought you loved me!"

4. When you do something unreasonable, always be ready with an excuse. Then you won't have to take responsibility. If you can't think of an excuse, look sorry and say, "I can't help how I am!"

5. Focus on the negative side of life. Then you can make yourself miserable and blame it on others.

6. Blame others for your mistakes. Then you won't have to feel responsible for your mistakes. Nor will you have to do anything about them.

7. Verbally attack those who criticize you. Then you don't have to bother listening to what they say.

8. Go along with the groups you are in. Then you won't have to figure out anything for yourself.

9. Act out when you don't get what you want. If questioned, look indignant and say, "I'm just an emotional person. At least I don't keep my feelings bottled up!"

10. Focus on getting what you want. If questioned, say, "If I don't look out for number one, who will?"

As you see, the list is almost laughable. And so it would be if these irrational ways of thinking didn't lead to problems in life. But they do. And often. Only when we are faced with the absurdity of dysfunctional thinking, and can see it at work in our lives, do we have a chance to alter it. The strategies outlined in this guide presuppose your willingness to do so.

This article was adapted from the book, *Critical Thinking: Tools for Taking Charge of Your Learning and Your Life,* by Richard Paul and Linda Elder. Criticalthinking.org Copyright ©2009 Foundation for Critical Thinking

MINI-ASSIGNMENT

In groups, discuss how your definitions compare with the definition presented in this article. What else did you learn about critical thinking from this article?

Chapter 2

The Writing Process

© alphaspirit/Shutterstock.com

TEN-MINUTE PROMPT

What is your writing process? What are some characteristics of a good writer?

In the last chapter, we discussed critical thinking and reading—reading with questions. Critical writing is the same thing—writing with questions. Every writer starts out with a question; every writer writes in response to something—a conversation, a book or movie, a major event or news story, another writer's op-ed piece. Writing is a *dialogue*—when you write, you are entering a conversation. But dialogue means more than just asserting your own opinions—it also includes listening and careful thinking. It means that when you write, you must connect your writing to the larger context or conversation—no one writes in a vacuum. Being a critical writer also means looking at your own writing critically—revising and editing objectively.

How do you generally write? If you're like most students, you sit down in front of the computer with a vague idea of what you want to write about, and you just start writing. You write until you fill the required number of pages, then maybe you read over it to check the spelling before printing it out and turning it in. Then you may have been surprised when you got a bad grade. That's because you didn't go through the process. Think about it—everything you do starts with small, basic steps, which you build upon. You wouldn't build a house without first making a blueprint; you wouldn't enter a basketball tournament without first mastering basic moves. Writing, like everything else, is a process that requires several steps.

The first thing you have to do before you start writing is to think about what you want to write. This may sound self-explanatory, but few people do it. Those who fail to plan ahead end up with rambling, disjointed papers that leave readers thinking, "Huh?" or, even worse, "So what?" So before you even sit down in front of the computer, put on your thinking cap and plan out your paper.

There are several things you need to consider before you start writing:

▶ **Purpose:** Why am I writing this? What do I want my readers to know/think/feel? How will they use what I tell them?

▶ **Audience:** Who are my readers? Who am I writing for? Will they find this useful or interesting? What prior knowledge do they have? In what context (academic, professional, personal) will they read my text?

▶ **Point of View/Angle:** How will I frame this topic? From what angle am I writing? How do I view this topic?

▶ **Voice:** How do I need to sound— do I want to sound serious, satirical, funny, inquisitive? How will my readers perceive me? This goes hand in hand with point of view; your voice is your presence in the text.

Why Ask about the Rhetorical Situation?*

Without a sense of audience and purpose, no one can write well. Inattention to the rhetorical situation results in disorganized memos that employees ignore or misunderstand, in public speeches that last too long and make an audience drowsy or restless, and in lectures that leave students confused.

When we ask about angle, we are looking for something of our own to say, a key point we will say more about shortly. If we find something we want to say, we are more likely to care about saying it well. If we have something to say, we also think about readers we want to reach. Connecting with them suddenly matters to us, so we care about how we sound. That is, we care about *voice.*

What Is Voice?

Voice refers to the writer's presence in a text, *how the writer "sounds."* When we read carefully, we can "hear" a person—a personality—in the words. Once again, the rhetorical situation determines how you want to sound. In informal social writing such as comments on a Facebook page, there is almost no such thing as too much personality. In other rhetorical situations, such as when writing a letter to a customer, the voice will sound more formal and reserved: Impatience, anger, and even humor in excess can be offensive in workplace communications. In some science writing an objective tone is appropriate. Voice varies according to the situation, but in all cases we should hear a person saying something that matters in a way that holds the reader's attention and is appropriate to the context and the genre of the text.

Read to hear the voice in each of the following two passages on the same topic, paleontology. The first is from a museum website at the University of California. The author is not identified. The second is from an essay published originally in the literary magazine *Harper's.* The author, David Quammen, writes with a concern for the environment.

The writer's voice reflects his or her stake in the topic.

Analyzing the Rhetorical Situation

These two excerpts are about the same subject, but they are very different. How do the two differ in tone? What is the intended audience for each? Where might you see these two descriptions published?

What Is Paleontology?

University of California Museum of Paleontology

...[P]aleontology is the study of what fossils tell us about the ecologies of the past, about evolution, and about our place, as humans, in the world. Paleontology incorporates knowledge from biology, geology, ecology, anthropology, archaeology, and even computer science to understand the processes that have led to the origination and eventual destruction of the different types of organisms since life arose.

Planet of Weeds

David Quammen

Hope is a duty from which paleontologists are exempt. Their job is to take the long view, the cold and stony view, of the triumphs and catastrophes in the history of life. They study the fossil record, that erratic selection of petrified shells, carapaces, bones, teeth, tree trunks, leaves, pollen, and other biological relics, and from it they attempt to discern the lost secrets of time, the big patterns of stasis and change, the trends of innovation and adaptation and refinement and decline that have blown like sea winds among ancient creatures in ancient ecosystems.

Why Does Voice Matter?

Learning to control the voice in your writing can increase your satisfaction with a writing project and improve your grade. A former student at the University of Hawaii, Monique Fournier, describes her discovery of the difference voice can make:

> *Six years ago, I dropped out of college after completing my sopho-more year. I assumed that it was because college wasn't for me, that I just wasn't meant for the classroom. It turns out that I wasn't ready for college writing. I now believe that once a writer finds her voice, she can easily apply it to any college-level writing assign-ment. Writing those first two years was difficult for me because I was simply plugging chains of words into every paper without any "me" glue to hold them together. Realizing I had a voice, and tak-ing steps to uncover it, has helped me (and my grade point aver-age) immensely.*

> —Monique Fournier, "Bees and Fears, Why I Write"[1]

Fournier realized that she had a voice and took "steps to uncover it." That sounds easy, but what steps did she take? Where does voice comes from?

To write with voice, we need the following:

▶ An angle, a point of view toward whatever we are writing about
▶ The courage to assert it

Writers adjust their voice to suit their purpose, topic, audience, and genre, but the essential question at the heart of writing with voice is, What stake do I have in my topic?

What Is an Angle?

What is this "me" that Fournier calls the glue that holds her words together? It comes from personal engagement, having a stake, in your topic. Writers often refer to this as "having an angle." For example, consider the two pas-sages on page 29 on paleontology. On the museum website, the writer's angle is the broad range of knowledge included in the modern study of paleontology. This angle promotes paleontology; it suggests that the reader might want to visit the museum or even take a course.

The other passage shows a darker angle on paleontology as the study of nature's indifference toward the plants and animals that have become extinct. Listing the specific objects that paleontologists study, the author shows his view of paleontology as a study of ancient mysteries. Not everyone would see it that way, but Quammen's angle shows his personal interest in the topic. In each case, the author has a point of view that gives voice to the writing.

A good way to think about angle is to compare writing with taking a photo-graph. Through your camera lens, you decide how to frame a scene or a person.

1. Dobrin, Sidney I., and Anis S. Bawarski, eds. *A Closer Look: The Writer's Reader.* New York: McGraw-Hill, 2003. 763. Print.

You may try out different angles, with different amounts of background, foreground, and contrast between light and dark. All of these decisions affect how you want to present your subject. Pictures show the photographer's angle on the subject.

Engaging with Topics: How Can I Find an Angle?

Whether you are writing about a social problem like bullying or a scientific topic like climate change, reflecting on your experiences and prior knowledge will help you find an angle, On any topic (represented here by "x"), questions that help to find an angle include the following:

- ▶ How does "x" affect me? Why does "x" matter?
- ▶ What is my opinion of "x"? What does it mean to me?
- ▶ What is the most interesting thing about "x"?
- ▶ How is "x" relevant to anything else I have observed or experienced?
- ▶ How is "x" relevant to anything else I have read about or studied?
- ▶ If I had to put "x" into a larger picture or category, what would that be?

*Source: From *Engaging Questions: A Guide to Writing* by Carolyn Channell and Timothy Crusius. Copyright © 2013 by The McGraw-Hill Companies, Inc. Reprinted by permission.

Let's practice using angle and voice. Take a look at these descriptions of the city Richardson, taken from their Convention and Visitors Bureau Website:

Meet Smart! Meet Richardson!

Richardson is the next place for your meeting or conference! Featuring 15 hotels offering 2,400 rooms, 203,000 square feet of total meeting and event space, 300 plus area restaurants, world class entertainment venues and the DART light rail system making visiting the local sights and sounds of Richardson or stepping out of the city to one of the many areas of interest such as museums, shopping malls and sporting arenas just a short ride away.

Visit Smart! Visit Richardson!

With its central location just north of Dallas and the popularity of its state-of-the-art performance hall, the Charles W. Eisemann Center, Richardson continues to be a favorite with visitors. Enjoy the multitude of professional, musical, dance, comedy and theatrical events not to mention the great award-winning festivals held throughout the year. As a result, Richardson enjoys an array of cultural entertainment that is virtually unsurpassed.

Richardson's extensive park and trail system enables visitors to enjoy a natural setting as well as a diverse set of recreational activities. Visitors to Richardson enjoy an outstanding selection of hotels, great shopping within minutes in every direction, restaurants to please any palate, a friendly atmosphere and a variety of entertainment options.

Courtesy of City of Richardson, TX Convention & Visitors Bureau.

As you can see, the details of each description differ depending on the audience. The first description is targeting businesses who want to hold a conference in Richardson, and the second targets tourists. Notice how the angle and the tone changes depending on which audience they are writing for. How might this be different if they were trying to attract college students?

MINI-ASSIGNMENT

Write your own "Discover Your Town." Your purpose will be to persuade people to either visit or live in your city. You will need to choose a specific audience to target (families, college students, gamers, hunters, etc.) and decide what angle and tone would work best for that audience. What details about the city should you highlight to attract this audience?

All of these elements tie into each other—who your audience is will inform your purpose, your voice, and your angle. Different purposes and contexts require different voices. For instance, a research paper for a history class requires a much more formal voice than a thank you letter to a friend.

Like critical thinking, writing is cyclical, not linear. Take a look at this flow chart:

Figure 2.1 Representation of the writing process.

As you can see, the stages of writing all flow out of, and into each other. This means that writing is more than just completing a linear set of steps. While there are distinct stages of writing, these stages are ongoing. For example, you may be in the process of writing a draft, and then find that you need to go back and reorganize, or gather more information, or rethink your purpose and audience.

There are four distinct stages in the writing process: **Brainstorming, prewriting, drafting, and revising.**

Start by thinking about your topic. Think about not only what you know, but what you want to know. Writing is about exploration, so don't just write to confirm your own opinions. Write to learn. Ask questions about your topic; look into your personal experience, and make connections to the larger context.

Prewriting is a crucial part of the process. It's very important to get your ideas out on paper so you can start organizing them into a formal paper. When you prewrite, don't think too hard. Save your judgment for the revising stage and just write your ideas without criticizing yourself. There are several strategies you can use: Outlining, webbing, listing, or free writing. Free writing is when you write continuously for ten minutes or so without stopping. This is also a useful brainstorming activity, as it can help you think about your topic. The purpose of the prewriting stage is to begin forming and organizing your main ideas.

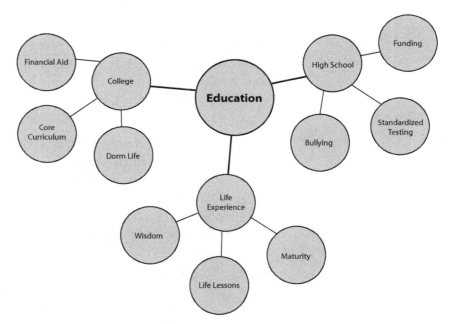

Figure 2.2   Example of a web or clustering.

Once you have considered all these points and organized your main ideas, you can start drafting. Where you start doesn't matter; don't think you have to start with the introduction and work in chronological order. You can start your paper anywhere you want. Think of it like putting together a puzzle—some people like to start with the corners, some like to start with the edges, but it doesn't really matter where you start as long as all the pieces fit together in the end to make a complete picture.

© vvoe/Shutterstock.com

JUST START WRITING! This is one of those subjects that you learn by doing and by practicing. So just start writing and see where it takes you.

Your next step will be to revise your paper for content; look at what your text says and how it says it. You may need to reorganize paragraphs, reword sentences, add detail, delete unnecessary or irrelevant information, etc. Revising is different than editing. When you edit, you look for things like punctuation mistakes or grammatical errors. This is important, but not as important as revising for content.

As you revise, ask yourself these questions:

- ► Is the thesis specific enough?
- ► Is the topic sentence fully developed in the paragraph?
- ► Do the body paragraphs need additional support, details, or examples?
- ► Does the writing contain information not relevant to the topic sentence?
- ► Do any sentences need to be moved to improve the flow of the writing?
- ► Are there sentences that need to be combined?
- ► Are transitions used to work the reader through the writing?
- ► Does the writing end with a sentence that gives a sense of closure to the paragraph?

As you edit, ask yourself these questions:

- ► Is the paragraph (or paragraphs) indented correctly?
- ► Do all sentences begin with a capital letter and end with some form of punctuation?
- ► Do all sentences contain a subject and verb and form a complete thought?
- ► Do all sentences have the necessary punctuation?

> ▶ Are words spelled correctly?
> ▶ Are verbs in the correct form?
> ▶ Do all subjects and verbs agree?
> ▶ Does the writing contain any run-ons, sentence fragments, or comma splices?

No one writes a great paper off the cuff. Even the greatest books ever written started out as a draft riddled with mistakes. If you take time to go through the process, to think about, plan, and revise your paper, you will become a much better writer, and writing will become a much more enjoyable activity.

© Andrew Krasovitchii/Shutterstock.com

Chapter **3**

Reflective Writing: Thinking Critically about Our Ideas and Experiences

"Reflective thinking turns experience into insight."

—John Maxwell

© De Visu/Shutterstock.com

TEN-MINUTE PROMPT

Respond to this quote:

"The unexamined life is not worth living."
—Socrates

What does he mean by this? What is the unexamined life? Do you agree or disagree?

We've started out by learning what critical thinking is, how it's done, and how it connects to writing and rhetoric. Now, let's start using what we've learned through practice and application.

This chapter is called "Reflective Writing." What does that mean? Basically, reflective writing is evidence of reflective *thinking*. In an academic context, reflective thinking usually involves:

- ▸ Looking back at something (often an event, i.e., something that happened, but it could also be an idea or object).
- ▸ Analyzing the event or idea (thinking in depth and from different perspectives, and trying to explain, often with reference to a model or theory from your subject).
- ▸ Thinking carefully about what the event or idea means for you and your ongoing progress as a learner and/or practicing professional.

Reflective writing is thus more personal than other kinds of academic writing. We all think reflectively in everyday life (as some of you do in your personal journals) but perhaps not to the same depth as that expected in good reflective writing at university level.

Reflective writing requires critical thinking. As we learned earlier, critical thinking starts with you. Before you can begin to assess the words and ideas of others, you need to pause and identify and examine your own thoughts. This involves revisiting your prior experience and knowledge of the topic you are exploring. It also involves considering how and why you think the way you do. The examination of your beliefs, values, attitudes, and assumptions forms the foundation of your understanding. Reflective thinking demands that you recognize that you bring valuable knowledge to every experience. It helps you, therefore, to recognize and clarify the important connections between what you already know and what you are learning. It is a way of helping you to become an active, aware, and critical learner.

Reflection offers you the opportunity to consider how your personal experiences and observations shape your thinking and your acceptance of new ideas. Reflective writing can help you to improve your analytical skills because it requires you to express what you think, and more significantly, how and why you think that way.

The Nature of Reflections

Here are some questions to ask yourself when beginning your reflective writing:

- ▸ **Topic:** What do I wonder about? A reflection focuses on one subject that opens up further avenues of thought.
- ▸ **Personal Connection:** How am I involved with my topic? Reflection demonstrates the writer's thinking process and ideas, so the writer refers to his or her thinking in the writing.
- ▸ **Details:** What examples and details help connect my thoughts with experiences? Reflections move back and forth between abstract thoughts and concrete experiences.

▶ **Conclusion:** Where has my thinking led me? A reflection is a journey; your thinking should take you to some destination or conclusion. Your ending should provide a sense of closure.

MINI-ASSIGNMENT

Has a small experience struck you as surprising, funny, or thought-provoking? This could be a conversation you had or an observation you made about human or animal behavior. Describe the experience, including the insight gained from it.

Student Sample Essay

Flores 1

Hesseltine 1

Summer Hesseltine

September 23, 2015

English 1301

Professor Hardin

The River of Life

Every once in a while, there is a moment in time when you realize that you

are completely present and aware of the world around you. These moments are rare

because it seems we worry so much about the future and forget to appreciate what

is happening right before our eyes. Sometimes, we come to discover what is truly

important in these priceless instances. I thought I understood what life was all

about; however, one evening at the Frio River this summer caused me to question

> Introduces the topic and establishes significance

Hesseltine 2

everything I thought I knew about what's important and gave me a new perspective

on what I want out of life.

      For as long as I can remember, my family has gone on vacation to the Frio

River in the summer; but this year, I had an experience that changed my

perspective. My family and I were sitting around our campsite overlooking the

river, just as we did every evening after dinner. The river, which had been full of

life just a few hours earlier, was calm and empty of people. The gently flowing

water was pellucid and I could see the rocks on the river bottom. Lining the

riverbank were towering cypress trees that were an enchanting shade of deep green.

As I looked further down the river, I could make out the luscious vegetation

bestrewn upon the rocky face of Mt. Old Baldy. The sun was just beginning to set

on the horizon, creating a vibrant red and purple masterpiece in the sky. The

summer heat had given way to a pleasant breeze, and the rustic smell of the

burning weed from our campfire filled my senses. The gentle rushing of the river

and the sound of locust singing faded into the background as the melody of my

brothers' laughter reached my ears. I don't recall exactly what they were laughing

about, for as I looked around at each of my family member's gathered in a circle,

all I could think was, "This is exactly where I am supposed to be." I was

surrounded by the people I love most in this world, in a place I hold dear to my

heart. I was fully there in the moment, and I felt a sense of contentment I still

cannot quite explain, as I realized memories like this would stay with me for a very

> Vivid
> descriptions

Hesseltine 3

long time. As I reflected on this experience later that night, I marveled at how alive I felt in that moment, though everything around me was so familiar and comfortable. I started to evaluate my mindset towards life thus far, and began to ponder what I wanted out of life moving forward. The main question that kept swimming around my head was, what really matters? If I had asked myself this question before, I probably would have answered naively. Now, I was thinking more abstractly and deeply about the world. I also started to question my priorities and thought about how easy it is to get distracted by the hustle and bustle of everyday life. It seems that many people in society are so focused on pushing forward to get ahead and achieving "success" in order to make a name for themselves. I am not saying these are necessarily bad things, for they are good aspirations; however, are they the most important things in life? In that serene moment with my family, surrounded by the beautiful natural world, those things really did not seem as important as they once did.

> Reflects on significance of experience

> Connects to a larger context

My exploration was full of insight and it made me realize that the seemingly insignificant moments like the one I experienced have the greatest impact. Yes, I want to be successful and I work hard every day to achieve the goals I have set for myself in the future; nevertheless, I want to enjoy all of the little moments that I won't get back. My worst fear is waking up one day and realizing that I spent so much time focused on preparing for the future that I let life pass me by.

Hesseltine 4

I am grateful for that evening at the river because it gave me a new perspective on life I had not really considered before. Instead of solely focusing on what lies ahead, I want to enjoy living in the present moment while I work towards the future. I do not want to lose sight of what I believe to be important because at the end of the day, relationships and the moments you share with people are what truly matter. The triumph felt at achieving success will last a good while, but the memories you make with people and places that mean something to you will be with you for a lifetime.

> Concludes by offering insights gained from experience

Student work reprinted with permisson.

The Assignment

Purpose

The purpose of a reflection is to think critically about experiences, ideas, and subjects, then reveal that thought process to your reader. Rather than try to persuade your reader, or simply inform them, your purpose will be to *get your readers thinking about your topic*, or to offer readers a space to think about experience. Your task is to explore your topic, connect your thoughts and experiences to a larger context, and demonstrate your thinking process.

Requirements

2–4 pages, MLA format

Guidelines

You have several options to choose from regarding topics:

1. **Reflect on a specific experience:** Sherman Alexie reflected on experiences he had in the educational system on the reservation, and that led him to think about how Native Americans are treated as stereotypes. You could choose to write about an experience you've had that led you to think about some deeper subject. You might also choose to

write about your educational experience; you could reflect on your journey to college, your previous writing experiences, or a specific event or person that impacted your education.

2. **Reflect on a specific subject:** What interests you? What do you think about? You could write about a specific topic that interests you, bothers you, makes you angry, or puzzles you. In this case, you will need to thoughtfully explore the subject, examine ideas and feelings related to it, and contemplate related subjects.

3. **Reflect on a piece of writing:** You could contemplate a book or another text that has impacted you or led you to think more deeply. However, this needs to be more than just a book report. Like the other options, you need to connect this to a larger context in order to open up further avenues of thought.

Whichever option you choose, your reflection must achieve the following:

1. Focus on one subject or experience that opens up further avenues of thought.

2. Connect your subject or experience to a larger context.

3. Explore questions, ideas, and connections related to your subject or experience.

4. Provide a sense of focus and closure—your questions and exploration should lead you to some destination, a main point that you want to make or ultimate question you want your readers to think about.

Organization

Your paper should have an introduction that introduces your topic or sets up the scene of your experience, and a conclusion that sums everything up. Other than that, the organization of a reflective paper is less formal than other pieces of writing. You may want to structure it something like this:

1. **Description:** what happened? What is being examined?

2. **Exploration:** discuss the most interesting aspects of your subject/experience, make connections to other subjects and a larger context, provide details, and examine ideas or feelings.

3. **Interpretation:** Where has your exploration led you? What have you learned from this experience? What do you want your readers to take away from this paper?

A Successful Essay Will

► Provide a critical reflection of a specific event or subject that reveals your thought process.

► Provide a conclusion that shows where your thinking has led you, and what this thinking reveals.

► Employ a logical and effective organizational structure of well-developed paragraphs, smooth transitions, and a strong introduction/conclusion.

► Engage the reader with interesting prose, good diction, and proper mechanics.

► Have an interesting title that relates to your paper's main theme.

Prewriting #1: Picking a Topic

1.   Make a list of five possible topics.

2.   Choose your top two topics and create a web on each. Look at the example in Chapter 2 for ideas on how to complete a web.

3.   Choose the topic you want to write about, and free write about it for five minutes.

Prewriting #2: Developing Your Ideas

1.   What are you going to write about? (Specifically, what will you reflect on?)

2.   Why are you reflecting on this? (What is your **purpose**?)

3.   What do you want your readers to take from this—what outcome do you want from this reflection?

4.   What **angle** are you taking, and what **tone** do you need to use?

5.   What details do you need to provide?

6.   What questions, connections, or ideas can you explore?

7.   How can you connect this to a larger context?

8.   How can you organize your ideas? (You might want to list your ideas or make an outline.)

Prewriting #3: Outline for Reflective Writing

I.   Intro

A.   Hook/opener.

B.   Transition to thesis.

C.   Thesis: What is the significance of this experience?

II.   Description

A.   Describe the experience.

B.   What details stand out to you?

III.   Exploration (Note: This section may take more than one paragraph.)

A.   What are the most interesting aspects of this experience?

B.   How can you connect this to other subjects and/or avenues of thought?

    C. How can you connect this to a larger context?

    D. Examine ideas/feelings related to this experience.

IV. Interpretation

    A. What insight did you gain from this experience?

    B. Where has your thinking led you?

    C. What do you want your audience to think about?

Chapter 4

Defining Concepts: Thinking Critically about the Language We Use

© IQoncept/Shutterstock.com

TEN-MINUTE PROMPT

Respond to this quote:

"Knowledge speaks; wisdom listens."
—Jimi Hendrix

What does he mean by this? How is he defining "knowledge" and "wisdom"? How are these two concepts different from each other?

One of the critical thinking questions we learned in the beginning of this book was, "What does that word mean?" That question may seem to have a simple answer, but in some cases it is not as easy as looking up a word in a dictionary. Many words we use every day have complex and abstract meanings. The meaning of many words is open to question. For example, during the Trayvon Martin trial, many people questioned what "justice" and "self-defense" meant. What constitutes self-defense? When does it cross the line to assault? Was justice served in this case? Many people disagree about these questions.

© Ivelin Radkov/Shutterstock.com

Here's another example: When someone claims that the Internet is the most democratic technology, what does that person mean by "democratic"? Is the Internet any more democratic than television or radio? In what ways? When we begin to question the meaning of these words, we begin thinking critically about statements that may initially pass as uncontroversial.

In this chapter, we will learn how to explore the meanings of words, especially concepts such as "democracy"—words that we use when talking about ideas that are important to us, and words that we use in many different ways and contexts. We examine concepts in an effort to understand what they mean and how they are used, often with some practical question in mind: Should flag burning count as "free speech"? Is the US truly a "democratic" country? Questions like these open the door for critical thought about issues that matter to us.

Take a look at the following chart from the Pew Research Center depicting the results of a survey of Americans who were asked what constitutes a family. What does this chart say about how Americans view family? How might this chart have been different 50 years ago? How might it change in the future? Who do you consider family?

What Is a Family?
% saying this is . . .

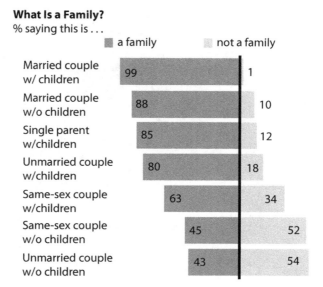

	a family	not a family
Married couple w/ children	99	1
Married couple w/o children	88	10
Single parent w/children	85	12
Unmarried couple w/children	80	18
Same-sex couple w/children	63	34
Same-sex couple w/o children	45	52
Unmarried couple w/o children	43	54

Note: "Don't know/Refused" responses are not shown.
Source: Pew Research Center

The Nature of Concepts

▶ **Concepts are abstract, not concrete.** For instance, Barbie dolls vs. Barbie culture. Barbie dolls are the concrete object, but Barbie culture is more abstract, implying the set of values associated with Barbie dolls and studied by sociologists interested in gender roles.

© Cylonphoto/Shutterstock.com

▶ **Concepts are often value-laden.** Concepts usually imply positive or negative judgments, sometimes both. For example, education generally has a positive connotation. However, one of the synonyms for education is brainwashing, which has a negative connotation. This means that some forms of education, which we usually think of in a positive way, can actually be negative.

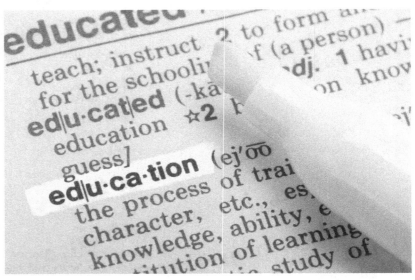

© Mega Pixel/Shutterstock.com

▶ **Concepts vary across cultures.** What is considered fashionable in Paris may be immoral in certain Islamic societies and just plain odd in American society.

© Richard Peterson/Shutterstock.com

▶ **Concepts vary across time.** As society's circumstances change, its concepts also change. For example, the word "innovation" used to mean something negative four centuries ago, implying the work of a troublemaker, whereas now we view the word as something positive, such as new and useful ideas.

We explore abstract concepts like "democracy" and "empathy" because their meanings are not so precise and limited. Understanding them better is important because such words belong to our value systems and affect the way we think and act. For instance, in his essay "What is Civility?" Forni explores the meaning of civility in order to understand how the word affects the way we treat each other.

MINI-ASSIGNMENT

In groups, explore the concept "education." Use the questions for exploring concepts to help you. How do these questions change your perception of what education means?

How Do Writers Explore a Concept?*

What should we ask when we want to think seriously about the meanings of a concept and its applications to life? Following are some basic questions that stimulate thinking about exploring concepts.

1. **What are the dictionary definitions of the concept?** Have definitions changed over time? Have the word's emotional associations changed, especially in a negative or positive direction? Four centuries ago, for example, "innovation" was a negative word, implying the work of a troublemaker, whereas now the word glows with all that is good and desirable.

2. **What are the root meanings of the word?** "Democracy," for example, comes from two Greek words meaning "people rule." It is not surprising, then, that "democratic" now means for many Americans much the same thing as "popular."

3. **In what contexts do people use the concept?** In one situation, "fairness" means that everyone gets an equal share of something—as even young children know when a treat is being distributed. In another situation, "fairness" means *unequal distribution,* as when one person or one group has contributed more than another to a successful enterprise and therefore deserves a greater share of the reward.

4. **Is conflict or disagreement at hand when the concept is used?** "Freedom" often runs headlong into "social responsibility." Smoking in enclosed public spaces was once common in the United States; now it is rarely permitted.

5. **What is the practical impact of the concept?** "Subprime mortgages" and financial contracts called "derivatives" so damaged the American and global economy that the investor Warren Buffett called them "weapons of mass destruction." Many people do not understand that file-sharing of copyrighted materials is "theft" in the same sense, as, for example, stealing someone's car.

6. **What company does this concept keep, and what distinctions are there among related ideas?** "Marriage," for example, connects with many other concepts, such as "soul mate," "monogamy," the "union

of a man and a woman," "reproduction," and so on. Increasingly the connected concepts are being separated from the institution as the institution itself changes.

7. **What have other writers said about the concept?** About "justice," for example, a Supreme Court justice famously said, "Justice too long delayed is justice denied." What is the relation of "justice" to "timeliness"?

8. **What confusions or uncertainties surround the use of the concept?** For example, the concept of "preemptive war" is used to justify a surprise attack on an enemy who is about to attack you. Can we distinguish between "preemptive war" as self-defense and the use of the concept to disguise a motive like expanding a country's territory by attacking a weak neighbor?

*From *Engaging Questions: A Guide to Writing* by Carolyn Channell and Timothy Crusius. Copyright © 2013 by The McGraw-Hill Companies, Inc. Reprinted by permission.

What Is Civility?*

P. M. Forni

Maybe I was coming down with change-of-season influenza. If so, I should really consider buying a little white half mask for my subway ride home.

—Sujata Massey

This reading comes from a best-setting book, Choosing Civility: The Twenty-five Rules of Considerate Conduct. *The author is a professor of Italian literature and civility at Johns Hopkins University, where he directs The Civility Initiative at Johns Hopkins. Before offering readers his "rules" for showing consideration toward others, Forni lays the groundwork by exploring the concept of civility.*

For many years literature was my life. I spent most of my time reading, teaching, and writing on Italian fiction and poetry. One day, while lecturing on the *Divine Comedy,* I looked at my students and realized that I wanted them to be kind human beings more than I wanted them to know about Dante. I told them that if they knew everything about Dante and then they went out and treated an elderly lady on the bus unkindly, I'd feel that I had failed as a teacher. I have given dozens of lectures and workshops on civility in the last few years, and I have derived much satisfaction from addressing audiences I could not have reached speaking on literature. I know, however, that reading literature can develop the kind of imagination without which civility is impossible. To be fully human we must be able to imagine others' hurt and to relate it to the hurt we would experience if we were in their place. Consideration is imagination on a moral track.

Sometimes the participants in my workshops write on a sheet of paper what civility means to them. In no particular order, here are a number of key civility-related notions I have collected over the years from those sheets:

Respect for others	Decency	Trustworthiness ,
Care	Self-Control	Going out of one's way
Consideration	Concern	Friendship
Courtesy	Justice	Friendliness
Golden Rule	Tolerance	Table manners
Respect of others' feelings	Selflessness	Lending a hand
Niceness	Etiquette	Manners
Politeness	Community service	Morality
Respect of others' opinions	Tact	Moderation
Maturity	Equality	Propriety
Kindness	Sincerity	Listening
Being accommodating	Honesty	Abiding by the rules
Fairness	Awareness	Compassion
Good citizenship	Being agreeable	Peace

This list tells us that

- ► Civility is complex.
- ► Civility is good.
- ► Whatever civility might be, it has to do with courtesy, politeness, and good manners.
- ► Civility belongs in the realm of ethics.

These four points have guided me in writing this book. Like my workshop participants, I am inclusive rather than exclusive in defining civility. Courtesy, politeness, manners, and civility are all, in essence, forms of awareness. Being civil means being constantly aware of others and weaving restraint, respect, and consideration into the very fabric of this awareness. Civility is a form of goodness; it is gracious goodness. But it is not just an attitude of benevolent and thoughtful relating to other individuals; it also entails an active interest in the well-being of our communities and even a concern for the health of the planet on which we live.

Saying "please" and "thank you"; towering our voice whenever it may threaten or interfere with others' tranquility; raising funds for a neighborhood renovation program; acknowledging a newcomer to the conversation; welcoming a new neighbor; listening to understand and help; respecting those different from us; responding with restraint to a challenge; properly disposing of a piece of trash left by someone else; properly disposing of dangerous industrial pollutants; acknowledging our mistakes; refusing to participate in malicious gossip; making a new pot of coffee for the office machine after drinking the last cup; signaling our turns when driving; yielding our seat on a bus whenever it seems appropriate; alerting the person sitting behind us on a plane when we are about to lower the back of our seat; standing close to the right-side handrail on an escalator; stopping to give directions to someone who is lost; stopping at red lights; disagreeing with poise; yielding with grace when losing an argument, these diverse behaviors are all imbued with the spirit of civility.

Civility, courtesy, politeness, and *manners* are not perfect synonyms, as etymology clearly shows. . . . Courtesy is connected to court and evoked in the past the superior qualities of character and bearing expected in those close to royalty. Etymologically, when we are courteous we are courtierlike. Although today we seldom make this connection, courtesy still suggests excellence and elegance in bestowing respect and attention. It can also suggest deference and formality.

To understand *politeness,* we must think of *polish.* The polite are those who have polished their behavior. They have put some effort into bettering themselves, but they are sometimes looked upon with suspicion. Expressions such as "polite reply," "polite lie," and "polite applause" connect politeness to hypocrisy, It is true that the polite are inclined to veil their own feelings to spare someone else's. Self-serving lying, however, is always beyond the pale of politeness. If politeness is a quality of character (alongside courtesy, good manners, and civility), it cannot become a flaw. A suave manipulator may appear to be polite but is not.

When we think of good *manners* we often think of children being taught to say "please" and "thank you" and chew with their mouths closed. This may prevent us from looking at manners with the attention they deserve. *Manner* comes from *manus,* the Latin word for "hand." *Manner* and *manners* have to do with the use of our hands. A manner is the way something is done, a mode of handling. Thus *manners* came to refer to behavior in social interaction—the way we handle the encounter between Self and Other. We have good manners when we use our hands well—when we handle others with care. When we rediscover the connection of *manner* with *hand,* the hand that, depending on our will and sensitivity, can strike or lift, hurt or soothe, destroy or heal, we understand the importance—for children and adults alike—of having good manners.

Civility's defining characteristic is its ties to *city* and *society.* The word derives from the Latin *civitas,* which means "city," especially in the sense of civic community. *Civitas* is the same word from which *civilization* comes. The age-old assumption behind civility is that life in the city has a civilizing effect. The city is where we enlighten our intellect and refine our social skills. And as we are shaped by the city, we learn to give of ourselves for the sake of the city. Although we can describe the civil as courteous, polite, and well mannered, etymology reminds us that they are also supposed to be good citizens and good neighbors.

Questions for Discussion*

1. Forni begins by arguing that learning to be kind to others is as important to a college education as learning about literature—or presumably any other area of academic study. Do you agree? If so, can kindness be taught? How?

2. A common way to explore concepts is to write about other closely related concepts. Forni offers a long list of other concepts associated with civility (paragraph 2). Does the list help you to understand civility better? Why or why not?

What is the Rhetorical Situation?

1. Who is the intended *audience* for this passage (and for the larger book)? Is Forni writing for students in an academic setting or for a more general public? Is he writing for people who are already well informed about notions of civility or for people who might not have thought much about the concept? Is there anything in this excerpt you can cite that implies the author's target readership?

2. A common way to explore concepts is to consider their etymologies, their root meanings or origins. Forni does this in his discussions of *courtesy, politeness,* and *manners.* Do the root meanings of these words, including *civility* itself, help you to grasp these concepts better? Why or why not?

Student Sample Essay

Flores 1

Lauren Flores

Professor Kimberley Hardin

English 1301

November 9, 2015

An Approach and Observation on Attitude

Attitude, according to Merriam-Webster, is defined as the way of thinking or feeling about someone or something; behavior that people regard as unfriendly, rude; or the arrangement of the part of the body or figure. This word was first used in the 17th century as a technical term in art, before developing the meaning of settled behavior reflecting feeling or opinion in the early 1800s, and finally, adopting the negative connotation of uncooperative and antagonistic from slang in the mid-1900s. As it was handed down, this word has varied from its original meanings, becoming a word of many definitions and perceptions according to the context which it is given, be it positive or negative.

The root origins of this word began with the Late Latin word altus—later known as aptitudinem—meaning "appropriate or fitting." It then was transferred to Italy, as the Italian word attitude, meaning "disposition or posture," and finally to French, to what we now know it as, attitude. Its current form originally referred to the posture of a figure in a statue or painting, but was later generalized to allude to the mental state as implied by the posture of the body. This change in definition

> Gives dictionary definition

> Etymology

> Thesis

> Tracks how the definition has changed

Flores 2

may have come about with the declination of art culture following the Renaissance,

leading to the association of it being a technical term in art to be lesser known.

When in use, I have seen this word most commonly applied as either its

negative connotation, in regards to bad behavior, or its more neutral connotation,

that in reference to emotion or feelings. I have also noticed that attitude is more

frequently remembered as its neutral connotation, rather than its other definitions.

cNoticeably, the "negative" definition of this word—that of being rude or

uncooperative—is displayed when it's in the opinion and convenience of the user.

That is, I've come to see it as a biased definition, such in that if this word is meant

to define a person's own feelings, then when, at what point, does the expression of

said feelings turn into that of rudeness and ill intention? An example of this

instance I find is very common between older and younger people. Each person

will verify their attitude as how they feel or think in consideration to a subject.

Many a time, these feelings will not be in agreement which the other person's,

resulting in conflict. When this happens, the younger may attempt to defend their

stance at the objection of the elder, who claims that the other is now behaving

poorly, and giving "bad" attitude. At that point, is attitude still a way of feeling,

or is it defiance? Even if the younger was defending a "good" attitude?

I've come to find that attitude in the negative form, is very often subjective,

and purely depends on these involved. Who am I to declare that a person is giving

bad behavior, lest they be reacting in an extreme form? In their head, they are

> Practical impact of the word

> Presents leading questions to explore

Flores 3

defending their own point of view, and in which, would that then make the accuser

the one with foul attitude? This particular point came to light when I was joking

with a friend, telling them to "stop giving me attitude" when they persisted that I

do something for them, though I had previously objected. This short fit was

childish at heart, but it made me realize how meaningless, and at times offensive,

disputes over attitude can be. Heading arguments with attitude being the main

offense has the implication that the other person's feelings are considered as trivial,

and results in a back and forth argument of trying to decide who is in the right.

Something which people, and I, often do not consider is how an attitude came

to be, how it formed; what history was made for it to come into existence. I would

presume that a major factor in what determines a person's attitude must be their

life experience; after all, it is through such occurrences that we are molded into

what we are today. Then, would it be possible that following this line of thinking,

we could come to an equation of: bad life experience equals bad attitude and vice

versa? We would also have to consider that often times, people are not so simple

and linear as to equate them to a single equation. In my life I have met people who

have faced unfortunate situations, yet their attitudes would be no indication of

such; similarly, I've met people who have experienced bad circumstances and

carried through to their attitude. Humans are diverse, so is it truly wise—or even

possible—to shorten their life to a single attitude which they express? It is the

> Gives real life examples

> Further explores the concept

Flores 4

easiest, definitely, but a single word, a single instance has not enough capacity to

define a person for who they really are, at their full length.

The very essence of attitude in society has seemed to have shaped many of its

social norms; determining how people view each other, how they interact, and how

they themselves develop. I believe that it has come to affect us in such a way that

we rely on its presence to deduct how we should proceed with our relationships

with other people. Good attitude for example, produces positive results: people are

happy, and are more inclined to view a person in a good light. Whereas bad attitude

produces negative results: it often leaves others in a similarly bad mood, and

creates an unfavorable image. In a way, we use these as social cues, as a sort of

one-word definition of goods and bad; thinking them to be definite truth despite it

only being only our own perception and impression of the person. Attitude, to

people, is a lasting impression which decides how others think of a person, and

how they act towards them.

> Discuss how the concept affects people

Attitude, I've come to learn, is complex. It has many definitions, which in turn,

branch out to many other possibilities. I can give a memorized definition—anyone

can—but accurately capturing the real impact that this single word has on society

is another thing. Attitude means behaving and displaying certain behavior, given

your circumstances; it means defending your opinion, even if it results in backlash;

it means being judged based on it alone. In this study and observation of the word,

I feel as if I have a greater understanding of the notion, that I've become aware of

> Concludes by summarizing results of the exploration

Flores 5

the interactions I have with others and how relationships and futures are impacted

as a result of these attitudes we put on for the world to see. It has also made me

realize that numerous concepts are not as black and white as they may be first

perceived to be; that there is almost always an underlying idea to be looked into,

and learned from. Attitude is but a function that we humans draw opinions from,

and act upon, all as an attempt of communication with one another.

Student work reprinted with permisson.

The Assignment

Purpose

Exploring a concept means thinking deeply and critically about the meanings of abstract words and their applications in real life. Words such as "democracy," "freedom," and "justice" are spoken every day, but their meanings are not so precise and limited. Rather than argue for a specific interpretation, your purpose for this paper will be to *explore* the different meanings, contexts, and applications of a concept.

Requirements

3–4 pages, MLA format

Guidelines

1. Remember that your primary purpose is to *explore,* **not** persuade. Your reader should see you as a thoughtful guide, and your paper should be *structured around questions* you ask yourself about the concept.

2. As your text says, the key to exploration is to *postpone closure*; therefore, you may end your paper by offering your specific understanding of the concept, but **only** after you have thoroughly explored it.

3. For your topic, draw from personal experience, class readings/discussions, foreign languages/cultures, or issues in your community. It's

best to choose nouns rather than adjectives (such as *friendship* or *friend* instead of *friendly*). Choose a concept that is not easy to define, the meaning of which has changed over time, cultures, or in different contexts, that can have both negative and positive attributes and applications.

4. Use the questions in this chapter to help guide your exploration. **You must incorporate at least four of these questions into your paper.**

5. Use online dictionaries, thesauri, and etymology Websites to help you gather information. You can also draw from other sources if you choose, but you must provide in-text citations and a Works Cited page.

Organization

1. Intro: Introduce the concept you intend to explore, provide the general or most popular meaning of the concept, and explain why it needs to be explored or rethought (this is your thesis).

2. Body: How you organize the body of your paper is up to you. You may organize it around sources, a set of questions, or your own stages of understanding. Just make sure the organization is logical, and that each point relates to and follows the next.

3. Conclusion: How you conclude will depend on your angle. You may conclude by providing your understanding of the concept, emphasizing the results of your exploration, challenging typical notions of your concept, or calling attention to questions that need further thought. Remember, you need not provide all the answers or resolve all the issues surrounding the concept.

Possible Topics

(Feel free to choose your own):

Manhood/Masculinity
Related TED talk: "A Call to Men" by Tony Porter

Womanhood/Femininity
Related TED talk: "Embrace Your Inner Girl" by Eve Ensler

Love and Sex
Related TED talks: "Sex Needs a New Metaphor" by Al Vernacchio
"Why We Love, Why We Cheat" by Helen Fisher

Education
Related TED talks: "Call to Reinvent Liberal Arts Education" by Liz Coleman
"Changing Education Paradigms" by Sir Ken Robinson

A Successful Essay Will

► Present a compelling and focused thesis that explains the significance of the concept.

► Provide an exploration of the concept through thoughtful questions about the definitions, contexts, problems, and applications surrounding it.

► Employ a logical and effective organizational structure of well-developed paragraphs, smooth transitions, and a strong introduction/conclusion.

► Engage the reader with interesting prose, good diction, and proper mechanics.

► Have an interesting title that relates to your paper's main claims.

Prewriting #1: Exploring a Topic

Write the word or concept you want to explore here: _____
_____

Now, start prewriting by filling out a **web**. Write your word or concept in the bubble, then brainstorm questions, issues, or related words or concepts to branch out into more bubbles.

Now go online and look up definitions, synonyms, and root words. Write them down here:

_____

_____

_____

_____

_____

Next, go to quotegarden.com or famousquotesandauthors.com and search for quotes about your concept. What have other (credible) people said about it? Write one or two interesting, discussable quotes here: (Remember to include who said it!)

_____

_____

_____

_____

_____

Prewriting #2: Generating Ideas

We've started by brainstorming ideas and gathering basic information about your concept; now, your task is to think more deeply about *implications of* the definitions, related concepts, and applications of the word. The following questions will help you generate ideas that you could use as main points in your paper.

1. **What is the definition and history of the concept?** Start with the definitions and etymology (the origins and history of a word) provided in a dictionary or online source, and consider the *implications and connotations* of them. For instance, the word empathy means the ability to feel what others are feeling; the connotations are almost always positive, implying a sensitive, caring person. Also consider how the concept has changed over time; the word family used to mean every person in a household, including the servants. How does that illustrate how the idea of family has changed over time?

2. **What other concepts are related to the concept you're exploring, and how are they related?** What synonyms can you think of that describe your concept? What are the *implications* of those words, and how are they different from your original concept? For example, a synonym for education (which has a positive connotation), is brainwashing (which has a negative connotation).

3. **What metaphors are used to describe your concept, and how do these metaphors influence people's perceptions of the concept?** Love is often compared to war; this metaphor could affect how people think of and act in relationships. Consider any metaphors attached to your concept and how they affect the way we perceive and act on it.

4. **Do different groups of people use the concept differently?** Your concept may mean different things to different types of people ("equal opportunity" for example, can mean one thing to those born into privilege, and something entirely different to those born into poverty). What conflicts or misunderstandings might result from these opposing views?

5. **How do people actually use the concept?** Consider how the concept is used and applied in real life. What is the practical impact of the concept in society?

Prewriting #3: Finding an Angle

Now that you have chosen and explored a topic, you need to *find an angle.* Your angle is your lens through which you view your topic; this could also be called your *point of view.* For instance, Cummins wrote about gender from the angle of perceived differences in gender and gender stereotypes; this led to his original question, "Are the sexes really different?" His point of view was that the way we perceive and define gender often "creates inequality and causes both men and women to be trapped in stereotypes."

Your task now is to figure out how you will frame your topic, then turn your angle into your starting point question. Think about these questions:

1. How does this concept affect me?

2. What does this concept mean to me? What is my opinion of it?

3. Why does this concept matter in a larger context?

4. What is the most interesting thing about this concept?

5. What context do I bring to this topic?

6. What outcome do I want for my explanation? What do I want my readers to understand about this concept?

Instructions

Complete this assignment on a separate Word document.

1. Choose three of the above questions and free-write about each one for five minutes.

2. Decide on a specific angle and turn it into a question. Your original question may start with "what is" (i.e., What is gender? What is civility? What is intelligence?), but then you will need to focus on a more specific question to pursue.

    Examples: What do the different perceptions of seduction imply about the nature of American and French cultures? Are gender differences innate or learned? Where do gender stereotypes come from, and how true are they? Why is civility important? Are there different types of intelligence?

3. Write down your point of view. As of right now, how do you view this concept? This point of view may change as you question and explore your topic further.

Chapter **5**

Proposals: Thinking Critically about Problems and Their Solutions

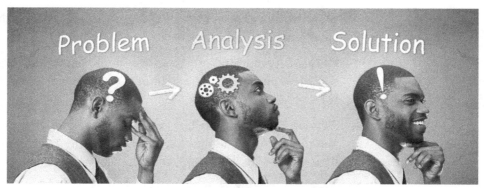

© PathDoc/Shutterstock.com

TEN-MINUTE PROMPT

What problems do you notice around your campus or town? What has been done to try to solve these problems? Have these solutions worked? Why or why not?

Problems surround us: The stray dog rambling down your street; the potholes you try to avoid while driving; the debt you incur while earning your degree. We are constantly facing problems and working to provide a solution to them. Some solutions falter, while others stand the test of time. This chapter is focused on identifying problems and finding reasonable solutions to them. A **proposal** is an argument (a **reasoned defense** of an opinion) that attempts to persuade readers to view a problem or an issue in a certain way, to convince them of the effectiveness of the proposed solution, and persuade them to take action according to the solution.

The Nature of Proposals

A proposal includes five aspects:

1. **Identify a problem:** Clearly define a specific problem that needs to be solved or addressed in some way. As you write your paper, you will probably need to focus on one aspect of the problem rather than trying to tackle the whole thing. For instance, in "Stop Marketing Foods to Children," Nestle started with the broad topic of obesity, then narrowed that down to childhood obesity, then looked for a root of that problem to narrow her focus to something manageable: Food marketing to children.

2. **Explain the problem:** What is the background of this problem? What are the negative effects? What else has been done to try to solve this problem? Why haven't those solutions worked? What is the scope and significance of this problem?

3. **Propose a solution:** What can we do to address this issue? Go into detail and provide specific steps or stages that we need to take in order for your solution to work.

4. **Defend your solution:** Use research to back up your claims, expect and refute counterarguments, and explain why your solution is better than what we're doing now or what has previously been proposed.

5. **Persuade people to take action:** This is called the "call to action" and usually appears in the conclusion. Ask yourself, what can the average person do to help? How can I encourage my readers to take action according to my solution?

© Keith Bell/Shutterstock.com

The Greek philosopher Aristotle defined three appeals that successful arguments use: Ethos, logos, and pathos. In order to persuade, you must:

1. **Convince readers of your credibility (ethos):** You make yourself credible by researching your topic thoroughly, using credible sources, and by sounding like an intelligent, reasonable person who is knowledgeable about the topic (in other words, your **tone**).

2. **Appeal to reason (logos):** This means you must be reasonable, use logic, and consider all sides of the issue. Refer back to the critical thinking strategies we discussed from the YouTube video and the article "Becoming a Critic of Your Thinking."

3. **Appeal to your readers' emotions and values (pathos):** Advertisers play on our emotions all the time to persuade us to buy a product or donate to a charity (think of all those ASPCA commercials featuring pictures of sad-looking animals in cages). David Dow appealed to his audience's emotions in his TED talk, "Lessons from Death Row Inmates," by giving us Will's personal story. By giving the problem a human face and invoking our sympathy for Will and people like him, Dow was better able to persuade his audience to see the issue from his point of view. Be careful with this aspect, though; you don't want to sound overly sentimental or melodramatic. Think about when it's appropriate to use pathos, and how you could effectively do so (without overdoing it).

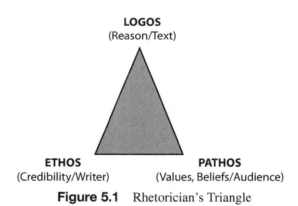

Figure 5.1   Rhetorician's Triangle

Example of a Proposal:

Stop Marketing Foods to Children*

Marion Nestle

From a public health perspective, obesity is the most serious nutrition problem among children as well as adults in the United States. The roots of this problem can be traced to farm policies and Wall Street. Farm subsidies, tariffs and trade agreements support a food supply that provides 3,900 calories per day per capita, roughly twice the average need, and 700 calories a day higher than in 1980, at the dawn of the obesity epidemic. In this overabundant food economy, companies must compete fiercely for sales, not least because of Wall Street's expectations for quarterly growth. These pressures induce companies to make highly profitable "junk" foods, market them directly to children, and advertise such foods as appropriate for consumption at all times, in large amounts, by children of all ages. In this business environment, childhood obesity is just collateral damage.

Adults may be fair game for marketers, but children are not. Children cannot distinguish sales pitches from information unless taught to do so. Food companies spend at least $10 billion annually enticing children to desire food brands and to pester parents to buy them. The result: American children consume more than one-third of their daily calories from soft drinks, sweets, salty snacks and fast food. Worse, food marketing subverts parental authority by making children believe they are supposed to be eating such foods and they—not their parents--know what is best for them to eat.

Today's marketing methods extend beyond television to include Internet games, product placements, character licensing and word-of-mouth campaigns—stealth methods likely to be invisible to parents. When restrictions have been called for, the food industry has resisted, invoking parental responsibility and First Amendment rights, and proposing self-regulation instead. But because companies cannot be expected to act against corporate self-interest, government regulations are essential. Industry pressures killed attempts to regulate television advertising to children in the late 1970s, but obesity is a more serious problem now.

It is time to try again, this time to stop all forms of marketing foods to kids—both visible and stealth. Countries in Europe and elsewhere are taking such actions, and we could too. Controls on marketing may not be sufficient to prevent childhood obesity, but they would make it easier for parents to help children to eat more healthfully.

Question for Discussion**

1. In Class, discuss "Stop Marketing Foods to Children." What is the problem the proposal would address? How does the author lead us to understand why the problem exists? How does she argue that no other solution except government regulation would work? What impact does she claim for her proposal if it were implemented? Do you find her reasoning persuasive? Why or why not?

Proposals are about trying to find new ways to do things. Writing a proposal requires a great amount of critical thinking and some creativity. Notice what other people have done in their proposals—they focused on a specific issue, and either narrowed the issue down to one aspect (as in Nestle's essay) or looked to the root of the problem to find a solution (as in David Dow's Ted Talk "Lessons from Death Row Inmates"). So, as you begin to explore problems and their possible solutions, think about what specific issue you could address, what angle you want to take (focus on one aspect or look to the root of the problem), and what could reasonably be done to help resolve this issue.

MINI-ASSIGNMENT

In groups, create a mini-proposal about one of the following subjects: sports (high school, college, or pro) education (primary, secondary, or college) or media (press/news or entertainment). Think of a problem within that subject and create a proposal addressing a possible solution. Be sure to hit all the aspects of a proposal.

The Assignment

Purpose

The purpose for this final paper is to think critically about problems and issues in society, then use rhetorical strategies of argument and persuasion to propose a solution to a problem. Your job will be to persuade your readers to view a specific problem or situation in a particular way, and take the action you propose. Remember, though, that this paper is not about proselytizing your personal opinion; it's about exploring all sides of a problem or situation through rational, open-minded investigation in order to reach a solution that adequately addresses the problem.

Requirements

3–5 pages, MLA format
At least three sources
Works Cited page

Guidelines

1. **Choosing a topic:** Problems are all around us, so finding a problem is easy. More challenging, however, is finding a problem that interests you, and one for which you can successfully advocate a reasonable solution. You may want to look for local issues around campus or your community, or look to the state or national level for problems. Remember, though, that many issues are too complex for a simple, wide-sweeping solution; so you may want to look at one aspect of the

problem (for instance, the economy is a very complex and multi-faceted problem, so you may want to focus on one aspect, like cutting spending or job creation).

2. **Brainstorming ideas and organizing your draft:** Ask yourself the following questions during your prewriting stage:

   a. **What problem am I trying to solve?** In your introduction, in addition to getting your reader's attention, you will need to clearly define the problem and explain its significance. (Why is this something that needs to be addressed? What are its negative effects? What could happen if we don't fix this?)

   b. **What is the background of this problem?** In your first supporting paragraphs, you will want to spend some time explaining the background of this problem, the roots of the problem, the causes and effects, and what else has been done to try to solve this problem (if anything).

   c. **What exactly am I proposing?** After you've explained the problem, you will need to present a clear and detailed outline of your proposed solution, including the specific steps necessary to actually make it happen.

   d. **How can I show that my solution will work?** As you outline your solution, you will need to show how and why your solution is a reasonable and adequate solution to the problem. You can do this by researching and using sources such as data and expert opinion to back up your claims, comparing your solution to others proposed to show why yours is better, and anticipating counterarguments.

   e. **How can I motivate my readers to take action?** In your conclusion, you will present a "call to action" to your readers to persuade them to take some sort of action to resolve the problem, according to your solution.

3. **Research:** You can look through newspapers and online news sites to brainstorm topic ideas, but for more in-depth research, you may need to go through the library's online databases. Your best bet is to go through EBSCO and Academic Search Complete, but you can also search for databases by subject. The sources you use should serve to back up your claims, not provide them for you, so you need to integrate sources in a way that supports your own ideas. You can use Google, but you must be very careful about the sources you select—make sure they are articles published by credible sources.

A Successful Essay Will

- ▶ Identify and define a specific problem.
- ▶ Present a compelling and focused thesis that fully explains your argument about the problem.

> ► Explain a reasonable and logical solution to the problem.
> ► Provide textual examples and evidence from other sources which support your assertions.
> ► Employ a logical and effective organizational structure of well-developed paragraphs, smooth transitions, and a strong introduction/conclusion.
> ► Engage the reader with interesting prose, good diction, proper mechanics, and an academic tone.
> ► Have an interesting title that relates to your paper's main claims.

Choosing a Topic: What can I write about?

Good topics for proposals are all around you:

> ► On campus, such as parking, dorm issues, or class scheduling.
> ► In your community, such as public transportation, caring for the homeless, and stray animals.
> ► In state level problems, such as public school financing, open-carry legislation, and teacher evaluation.
> ► In national level problems, such as wars, the national debt, and financial aid.

As stated earlier, you probably do not want to take on a very large problem like world hunger. If you choose a complicated problem, such as child labor in developing countries, a proposal for what a single company could do would work better than a sweeping solution for the entire problem. Large scale problems require complex, multi-faceted solutions that you may not be able to write about adequately in a short paper. Focusing on one small aspect of a big problem will prove more successful.

If you're having trouble choosing a topic, consider the following:

> ► **Recent news:** What's happening in your town, your state, the country, or the world? What's making the headlines? Looking through print or online newspapers can bring your attention to problems you may not even know existed.
> ► **Problems around campus or town:** What problems have you noticed that other people don't seem to be aware of?
> ► **Your own interests:** Maybe you are interested in animal rights, environmental causes, child welfare, or gun control. The subjects you are already involved in can be good places to begin.

As you prepare your solution, you need to think about the following:

> ► **Contributing factors:** Sometimes the solution to a problem focuses on changing the factors contributing to the problem rather than the problem itself. For example, Nestle's essay focused on one of the factors contributing to childhood obesity, food marketing.
> ► **Root causes:** In other cases, a proposal will focus on the root of the problem. For instance, David Dow focused on one of the roots of murder, juvenile delinquency, as a solution to preventing people from

ending up on death row in the first place. Rather than argue about whether or not the death penalty is permissible or effective, he looked to the root of the problem to try and solve it from the ground up.

► **Previously attempted solutions:** Research what has already been done to address your problem, and identify what has and has not worked. Then you can show why your proposal is the best solution to the problem.

► **Controversies surrounding your topic:** If your problem is a controversial one, such as abortion or the death penalty, consider all sides carefully, and think about how your solution can appeal to all sides.

Prewriting #1: Brainstorming Problems and Solutions

INSTRUCTIONS

The first step for this paper is brainstorm possible topics. Think of three problems that could be possible topics, brainstorm three different possible solutions, and finally, evaluate whether or not the solution would work. Ask yourself some critical thinking questions to help you come up with and evaluate possible solutions (use the example below as a guide). If a solution is possible, how might it work? What would we have to do to make it work?

EXAMPLE

Problem #1: Gun Violence	Solutions	Evaluation
Possible solution #1	Make guns illegal.	Not possible; against the Constitution.
Possible solution #2	Increase background checks, limit ammunition and ban certain types of guns such as assault weapons.	Possible, but legislation on this already failed. Could we try this again? If so, how?
Possible solution #3	Require everyone purchasing a gun to register the weapon and take a gun safety course.	Possible, but some may argue that this infringes on their rights, and we wouldn't be able to enforce this for weapons bought at gun shows and private sales between individuals. Could we alter or combine this with another solution to make it work?

Prewriting #2: Brainstorming a Topic

1. Now that we've done some brainstorming, decide on a specific problem you want to discuss. Write the issue in the space below.

2. What do you already know about this issue?

3. What do you *need* to know (what will you research?)?

4. Whom does this issue affect? Why is this a problem? What are or could be the negative effects? What are the *roots* of this problem (your solution may focus on the root of the problem and not the problem itself)?

5. What have other people done or said to provide a solution to this issue? How well have those solutions worked? If they haven't worked, why not?

6. What solution will you propose? Why is your solution the best one? How will it work?

7. What action do people need to take in order for your solution to work?

8. Now that you have done some prewriting on your topic, you need to focus on a specific problem within that topic. For instance, you may have started with the broad topic of issues in college education. Then, you decided to focus on financial issues; that can lead to your specific problem of rising tuition costs. In order to narrow the focus of your paper, first take your problem and turn it into a question. Instead of expressing as an issue ("Should _____"), express as a problem with the verb "How can _____?" as in "How can we make college more affordable without sacrificing quality education?" The answer to this question will eventually become your thesis statement.

Write your question here:

Proposal Prewriting #3: Focusing on a Specific Problem

1. **Testing your problem:** Select the exact question you want to work with, and test it by the following criterion. (Now's the time to change your mind, not later.)

    ▶ Is the problem a "social" problem rather than a personal one?

    ▶ Does the problem have magnitude? Does it not only affect you personally, but a larger community for whom the stakes are high? (Example: "How can my sorority attract more members?" might be important, but lacks magnitude.)

    ▶ Is the problem narrowed and focused enough? You don't want too much magnitude. Example: "How can we solve world hunger?" That's way too broad. If the problem is too big to be solved all at once, try to divide it into several related problems, or look to the roots of the issue.

2. **Steps of solution:** Write down the major steps, or stages, necessary to carry out this solution—Your specific steps of action to make the solution happen. Be thorough and precise. This is the key element of the essay, and distinguishes your proposal from your solution. The job of the proposal is to make the solution happen. Remember, your solution may have more than one element to it.

3. **Defending your solution:** Write a few sentences refuting each of the following statements:

   ► We can't afford it.

   ► It would take too long.

   ► Few people would benefit.

   ► We already tried it, and it failed.

4. **Listing reasons**: List every possible reason you can think of that might help convince people to believe in your proposal.

5. **Choose your strongest reasons**: From your list in the previous questions, state your three strongest reasons to support the strength of your proposed solution.

Chapter 6

Why Do Research?

Research is an essential part of writing, and a big piece of your proposal. But why use other sources in the first place? First of all, doing research gives you more knowledge about your subject; and the more knowledgeable you are, the better your paper will be. Second, using sources helps you put your arguments in context. In the beginning of this book, we learned that writing is a conversation; by reading what others have said and responding in your own writing, you are entering that conversation. Finally, using sources makes you a credible writer; if your readers can see that you have researched this subject and used credible sources, they are more likely to listen to what you have to say. In short, doing research makes you a more knowledgeable, credible writer who joins a community of other writers.

© Rawpixel/Shutterstock.com

Research begins with questions, not just a topic. Without questions, research would be an aimless task. There is one major question to ask when starting research: Given what I already know about this topic, what do I *need* to know? Asking this critical question reveals gaps in your knowledge and shows you what you need to focus on when researching.

Research is more interesting and creative than just gathering facts. Research helps us ask and answer a more important question: What do the facts *mean*? This question requires critical thinking, which leads to more questions and answers. For instance, while researching teenage pregnancy, you might find that the states who teach abstinence-only sex education have higher rates of teenage pregnancy. What does this fact reveal about sex education programs? It's your job as a writer to analyze the facts you've gathered and incorporate them into a meaningful and cohesive paper.

How Do I Find Sources?

When writing an academic paper, you want to look for academic sources; that's why your best bet is to go through your library's database. The library database has dozens of search engines on multiple subjects, and all the resources are academic and **peer-reviewed.** That means that the articles submitted to the journals were reviewed and fact-checked by a group of professionals in that field. You know you're getting reliable information from a library database.

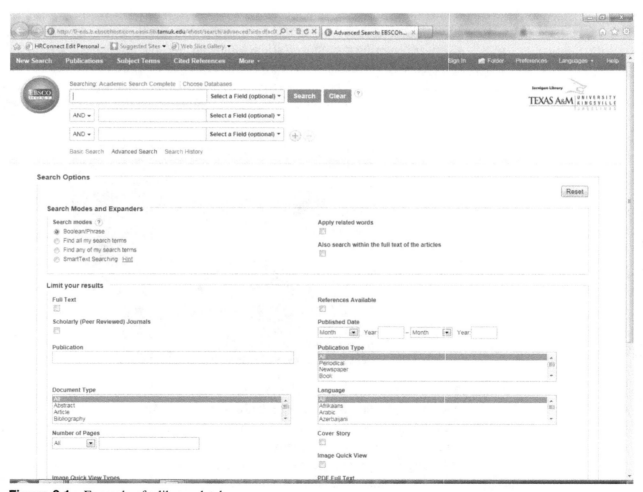

Figure 6.1   Example of a library database

Searching on a database is different from searching on Google; on Google, you can type in a whole sentence or question, and it will find results for you related to that question. But if you search for a whole sentence in a library database, it will search for that exact sentence within an article, and most likely will not find it. That's because library databases search using **Boolean operators.** These are words (AND, OR, and NOT) put in between keywords to refine search results. A library database automatically searches with the Boolean operator AND, which means it searches for every single word you type. That's why you need a set of **keywords** handy.

Boolean Operator	Explanation
AND	Narrows your search. Use with different concepts. Example: (gas-powered cars) AND (electric-powered cars).
OR	Broadens your search. Use to search for sources using one or more synonym. Example: (electric cars) OR (fuel cell cars).
NOT	Narrows your search. Use to eliminate irrelevant material. Example: (gasoline-powered cars) NOT (natural-gas powered cars).

Figure 6.2   Boolean operators

Keywords are a set of words that are commonly used to describe your topic. Start generating a list of keywords by looking at your research question for words that describe your topic. For instance, if you're writing a research paper about the effects of school budget cuts on student learning, you could start with the basic keywords "education budget cuts." Add words you encounter while researching as well as synonyms and related concepts. If you don't find what you're looking for with one set of keywords, try using another: "school financial reform" instead of "education budget cuts," or, even more specifically, "effects of education budget cuts." Keywords should be specific to your topic to avoid receiving irrelevant results. For example, if you just search for "education," you would get thousands of results that have nothing to do with budget cuts, and it will take you longer to filter through them. Most search engines allow advanced searches that limit results by date, type of source, or other criteria; this will allow you to even further narrow your search results.

Remember when you do research, you need to:

1. Be patient—it takes time to filter through results, find relevant sources that can add to your paper, and figure out how to incorporate them into your paper. Don't get discouraged if you don't find anything the first time you search; keep at it and you will find something.

2. Be persistent—if you don't find any results from one set of keywords, try a different set of keywords. Keep trying different keywords, databases, and search engines until you find what you're looking for.

3. Be smart—read your sources critically; think about how your source can add to your paper. Start with your own ideas and arguments, then look for sources that can back up your claims.

© wavebreakmedia/Shutterstock.com

How Do I Evaluate Sources?

While library databases are the best way to find academic sources, you may also choose to find more popular sources through Google. You have to be especially careful when searching on Google; you must be able to evaluate a source to see if it's reliable.

Evaluating a resource from a library database is easy; begin by reading the **abstract,** the brief summary of the article. This will allow you to see if the content of the source is relevant to your paper without having to read the whole article. Note the source where the article is published, and the date it was published. Remember that you can limit your search to a certain time frame; this will help you avoid sources that are outdated. Remember, for a source to be useful to your specific paper, it has to fit well with your topic and purpose.

Evaluating on online source is more difficult, because the results haven't been handpicked from professional, peer-reviewed journals. You need your critical thinking and reading skills to evaluate an online source. First, read critically:

► What arguments does the author make?
► What reasons and evidence does the author give to support his/her claim?
► How thoroughly did the author explore opposing arguments?
► Do you agree or disagree with the author's claims, or do you agree with one part while disagreeing with another? Why do you agree/ disagree?
► What is the author's stance, his/her attitude towards the subject? Does the author attempt objectivity, or does the argument seem biased? Is the author affiliated with some special interest group/organization that may affect the author's perspective? What assumptions does the author bring to the text?

Think about the authors themselves: what makes them a reliable source on this subject? Look for an author's **credentials**, their qualifications such as degrees and work experience. If you can't find any information on the author, or if the author is not an expert in the field they're writing about, it may not be a reliable source to use.

Then, think about the source itself:

► Is it RELEVANT? Does it relate to your purpose? Will it add to your work?

► What kind of source is it? Is it a book, magazine, journal, newspaper, website?

► Is it SCHOLARLY and PEER-REVIEWED?

► If it is a journal or magazine, is it REPUTABLE? Which of these magazines is more reputable: *National Geographic* or *Cosmopolitan*?

► Newspapers should be reputable too—*The New York Times* or *Star*?

► Nonfiction books should attempt to be unbiased and based in facts, not personal opinion. A book that takes a specific side is fine, as long as they use facts and evidence to back up their claims.

► Bibliographical information: Does this source use other sources that are scholarly? Is there a bibliography? Are these sources reliable? If you can't find where an author got his or her information, it may not be reliable.

► Date of publication: Consider when the source was published. If you are writing a research paper on the importance of sex education in middle school, for example, you might not want to quote an article written in the 1950s, because too much has changed since then for that source to be relevant.

Evaluating Websites

► **What is the domain name extension?** You can use a website's URL to help you judge reliability. Some common domain types are:
  - Commercial (.com and .net): These sites include businesses and their publications and other commercial publications. Web magazines, personal webpages, and blogs also end in .com.
  - Nonprofit organizations (.org): These sites include charities and advocacy groups, such as ASPCA.org, an animal rights group that advocates against animal abuse through various services and programs. Be aware, though, that the use of this extension is open to anyone, so the fact that a website ends in .org does not guarantee that the site is operated by a nonprofit or that it is reliable. Keep in mind as well that some organizations are biased, meaning they take a specific side on issues. An example of this is Americasvoice. org, a left-leaning organization dedicated to immigration reform. Since some nonprofits lean to the right or to the left, be aware of bias in their writings. It's best to gather sources from all different sides so you get a complete picture of the issue.
  - Educational institutions (.edu): These are associated with schools, colleges, and universities, including the pages of individuals associated with these institutions.

■ Government agencies (.gov or .mil): These sites are useful for gathering the latest information about any aspect of American government.

© YanLev/Shutterstock.com

In general, sources found on educational and government websites are most likely to be reliable. However, an article posted on an educational website could be a student paper, so you always need to look further into the source. Sources with the domain name extensions .org, .com, .net, or .biz need to be carefully evaluated to determine if they are credible.

There are several questions to ask when evaluating websites:

► **Who is the publisher?** A website that serves as the official online presence of a reputable company, nonprofit, or school is likely to be reliable. You will need to use critical thinking and reading skills to determine which websites are legitimate. One way to verify this is to consider how you arrived at the website; being directed to a site from a source you already trust indicates that the site is reliable. Be wary of any site for which you cannot determine the publisher.

► **What is the purpose of the website?** Websites of reputable institutions and organizations will provide information about their mission, programs, and funding through the "About Us" section. Think carefully about an organization's agenda when deciding if it's a reliable source. If you can't find any information about the organization's mission or purpose, it may not be reliable.

► **Do the authors have appropriate credentials?** Sometimes a website will put biographical information about their authors on the website; usually this is done by creating a link to the author's name in the byline. If you click on the author's name, it should take you to a page describing the author's other achievements. Check every author's credentials to ensure he or she has some authority on the topic. If you don't know who wrote it, it may not be reliable.

► **Has the website been recently updated?** Look for the most recent copyright date, usually located at the very bottom of the page. Avoid websites that have not been updated in over a year, because they may be abandoned or neglected. Also avoid websites that offer undated information.

► **Has the author cited sources?** Look for a bibliography, a works cited, or footnotes that tell you where the author received his or her information. Sometimes these sources are listed with links that take you to the original source. If you don't know where an author got his or her information, it may not be reliable.

How Do I Incorporate Sources?

When you incorporate sources into your paper, you join a conversation that includes ideas and information from the sources you cite, your interpretation of what other people are saying about your topic, and your presentation of your own views. To use your sources well, you must not use them in isolation, but blend them, a critical thinking skill known as **synthesizing**, which means *bringing together.* A good research paper uses multiple sources within one section, even within one paragraph. As you read your sources, use annotations to note where authors talk about the same topics. Notice areas where they agree or disagree; it is possible that sources may contradict each other, and this is also worth noting and pursuing in further research. We incorporate sources into our papers by **quoting** or **paraphrasing**.

The Art of Quoting

Quoting others is an essential part of writing, but there is an art to it that many are not experienced with. Quoting can add richness and complexity to your papers, but doing so incorrectly can ruin them.

One of the biggest mistakes people make regarding quoting is to allow the quotes to take over their papers. Quotes should enrich your own writing, not write for you; they should support your own ideas, not supply them. The art of quoting requires a balance between what you say and what they say. The best defense against this kind of mistake is to begin with your own ideas, then look for quotations that support or expand on them; in other words, don't look for quotes to GIVE you ideas, look for quotes that RELATE TO your ideas. Think about relevance; ask yourself how a quote will support one of your particular points.

Another common mistake occurs when writers provide quotes, but fail to provide an explanation of them; such writers assume that the meaning of the quote, and its connection to the rest of the paper, is obvious to the reader, because it seems obvious to them. Remember, your readers can't see inside your head; you can't expect them to make all the connections you made in the process of writing, because they haven't gone through that process.

So the goal for quoting, then, is to first provide relevant passages that back up your own ideas, and then to explain their meaning and significance to your reader. You can do this fairly easily through a strategy called "sandwiching": introduce the quote, provide the quote, explain the quote. Integrate the quotes into your text, and provide your interpretation. This builds a bridge from the source to your own text.

Introduce → Quote → Explain

Example

[*introduce*] Graff protests against writers who quote sources without providing any explanation for them. [*quote*] He claims, "Such writers fail to see that quoting means more than simply enclosing what 'they say' in quotation marks" (43). [*explain*] In other words, simply putting a quote into a paper isn't enough; a writer must also explain what the quote means in the context of their own ideas.

Probably the most difficult aspect of quoting is integrating them into your text, both in content and in format. Some people think all quotes must be in the same format, usually this one: According to So-and-So, "Blah blah blah." You don't always have to set up your quotes this way; in fact, you don't necessarily need to provide the name of the person you're quoting within the sentence (that's what in-text citations are for).

There are different ways to quote, and each way requires a different format. Quotes that are specifically introduced should always be set apart with commas.

▶ Learning to quote sources is not cut and dry. As the text book states, "not all quotations require the same amount of explanatory framing" (Graff 49).

The only exception is if you use "that" in place of the comma.

▶ Learning to quote sources is not cut and dry. The text book states that "not all quotations require the same amount of explanatory framing" (Graff 49).

A more sophisticated style of quoting allows the writer to incorporate a few words or a phrase into their own sentence. This is a good way to avoid overly long quotes and to blend your own voice with some key phrases from the source. When you blend paraphrase and direct quotations so that the quoted words are integral to your own sentence, no punctuation is needed to set off the quoted words:

> ► The realization that our structures of history and reality are ineffective leads to the "indeterminacy of knowledge," encouraging us to "question whether this story, or any story, can know, or ever claim to know," the Truth (Horne 146).

Another example of formatting:

Many still denounce Family Guy as bigoted and crude. New York Times journalist Stuart Elliot claimed just this year that "the characters on the Fox Television series Family Guy...purposely offen[d] just about every group of people you could name."

> ► The author used an ellipses (...) in the middle of the quote because she skipped over words she thought were irrelevant to her sentence.
> ► She used brackets around the d in offend because she changed the tense to fit her own sentence. The original source probably said "offended."
> ► Main point: The quotes should serve to enhance your own thoughts, so fit them around your own words.
> ► Finally, notice that instead of just saying "Stuart Elliot claimed," the writer identifies him as a journalist and provides his credentials. If the writer hadn't done this, we'd have no idea who Stuart Elliot is, and might be less inclined to listen to his claim.

Sometimes, a longer quote is needed. If it is longer than 4 lines, set the quote apart on its own line, indented twice. This is called a "block quote."

Example:

One newspaper interview reveals Blackstone's ulterior motives for becoming a musician:

> I want the American people to know the Indian as he is and has been, and not as he has been so grossly misinterpreted to be . . . . Indian traditions and traits of character have been monstrously defamed. The popular conception seems to be drawn largely from motion picture characterizations. I feel in justice to my people that I should do all in my power to dispel these illusions. (qtd. in Troutman 238)

Block quotes do not use quotation marks, and the end punctuation goes before the citation, not after. They should only be used if every line has some relevance to your ideas; and, of course, they should be fully explained.

How Do I Cite?

When you quote or paraphrase someone in your paper, you have to provide a citation called a parenthetical. The citation includes the author's last name and the page number where the quote can be found; this info is given in parenthesis AFTER the quote and BEFORE the period.

> ► Example: "Quote" (Smith 49).

- ► However this also depends on how you incorporate the quote:
  - With Author in Text: Voltaire's character Candide is startled upon learning that this man did not own "an enormous and splendid property," but rather a mere twenty acres that he cultivates with his children (76).
  - Without Author in Text: Candide is startled upon learning that this man did not own "an enormous and splendid property," but rather a mere twenty acres that he cultivates with his children (Voltaire 76).
  - If there is no author, cite the title of the work (the first couple of words): Statistics indicate that drinking water can make up 20 percent of a person's total exposure to lead ("Information" 572).
  - If there is no page number, as in an internet source, simply put the author or the title of the web page: Starbucks has been a major force for ethical conservation in the business world. According to their website, Starbucks employs "a holistic approach to ethically sourcing coffee through responsible purchasing practices, farmer loans and forest conservation programs" ("Responsibly Grown").

How Do I Do a Works Cited Page?

Works Cited pages are complicated, mostly because they are very detail-oriented. All Works Cited entries have the same information in them, in the same order:

Last name, First name. Title. Publication information.

But the details change depending on what kind of source you use. If you're using a source from the library database, your Works Cited entry will look like this:

Last name, First name. "Title of Article." *Title of Journal,* vol, issue, date, page numbers. *Database.* DOI or URL. Access date.

Matt, Willie. "Taxing and Tuition: A Legislative Solution to Growing Endowments and the Rising Costs of a College Degree." *Brigham Young University Law Review,* vol. 2012, no. 5, 2012, pp. 1665–1704. EBSCO. http://0-eds.a.ebscohost.com.oasis.lib.tamuk.edu/ehost/detail/detail?vid=3&sid=74bf98a4-f628-4f20-8368-53fe6419b9b4%40sessionmgr4009&hid=4205&bdata=JnNpdGU9ZWhvc3QtbGl2ZQ%3d%3d#AN=85445692&db=a9h8. November 2014.

If you were to quote this source in your paper, it would look like this: "Quote" (Matt 1667).

An article from a publication that you found online may look like this:

Last name, First name. "Title of Article." *Name of website.* Publisher of

website, Date, URL, Access date.

Lewin, Tamar. "Annual Rise in Cost of Public College Slows."

Nytimes.com. The New York Times Company, 23 October 2013,

http://www.nytimes.com/2013/10/23/education/annual-rise-in-cost-

of-public-college-slows.html, Accessed 8 November 2014.

Since there are no pages for this source, your in-text citation would look like this:

"Quote" (Lewin).

Websites are different and more difficult. A web*site* is different from a web-*page*; the webpage is like the article in a journal, and the website is like the journal. It can also sometimes be challenging to figure out who the author and publisher are. Generally, the publisher is the organization of the website itself (so the publisher of the New York Times website is The New York Times Company). If you're not sure who published the website, look at the bottom of the page for the copyright. If you can't find a publisher, then it may not be a good source to use. If there's no author listed, then you just start with the name of the webpage. Here are a couple of examples:

Last name, First name (if no author, skip this). "Title of Webpage." *Name*

of Website. Publisher of Website, Date, URL, Access Date.

"Tuition Inflation." *FinAid.org.* FinAid, 2013, http://www.finaid.org/

savings/tuition-inflation.phtml, Accessed 8 November 2014.

"Tuition and Fees Refund Policy." *Tamuk.edu.* Texas A&M University

Kingsville, 6 May 2011, https://www.tamuk.edu/schedule/refund.

html, Accessed 8 November 2014.

Since these sources have no author, you would use the title in your in-text citation:

"Quote" ("Tuition and Fees").

"Quote" ("Tuition Inflation").

There are many different types of sources, all with different details. You will need to use a guide when writing a Works Cited page. A good source to use is Purdue University's online writing lab (OWL); you can find this by Googling "OWL Purdue MLA." Allow yourself plenty of time to write your Works Cited page. This is not something to do at the last minute! A few things about Works Cited:

1. They are in ABC order.
2. If it's an online source, you must include your access date (the first date you found the source).
3. The entries are double spaced, and every subsequent line is indented.
4. Pay special attention to punctuation.
5. Titles of books, journals, magazines, and newspapers always go in italics. Titles of the articles within them always go in quotation marks.
6. The last name of the author always goes first; if there are two authors, you list them like this: Smith, John and Jane Doe.
7. If there are more than you two authors, you do it this way: Smith, John, et al. ("et al" means "and others").

8. With web pages, the publisher is usually the name of the institution/organization affiliated with the site. For example, the publisher of CNN.com is CNN.
9. Remember the difference between a web SITE and a web PAGE: A web site usually has more than one web page. So the pages on a website are like the articles in a journal; you have to cite each one separately. Say you used Starbucks.com as a source, and you quoted from both the "About Us" section and the "Products and Services" section. Each of those sections is a separate webpage on the site. So your citation would look something like this: "About Us." Starbucks.com. Starbucks, Inc. 2012. Web. 15 November 2012. OR "Products and Services." Starbucks.com. Starbucks, Inc. 2012. Web. 15 November 2012.
10. The Works Cited is the last page in your paper. So if your paper is 4 pages long, the Works Cited is page #5.

If you're researching through a library database, all the information you need is there:

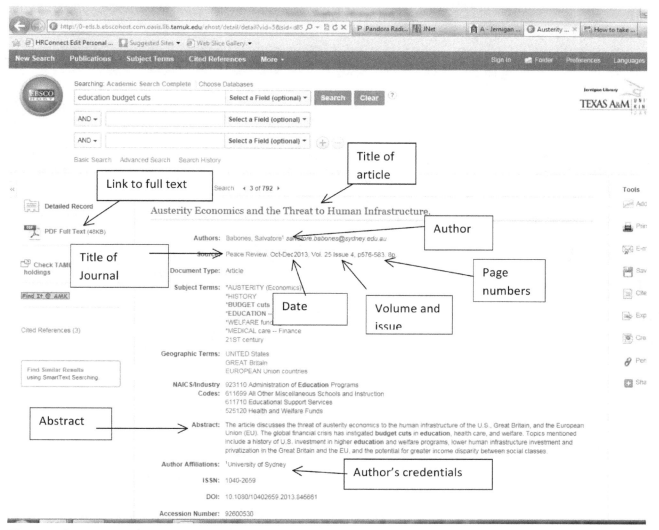

Figure 6.3   Anatomy of a Database Article

Chapter **7**

Style Guide

All Those Rules versus the Four Basic Sentences

If you're like most writers, editing your punctuation can seem pretty intimidating. Where do you start? Every sentence looks different. And what about all those rules? Comma rules are a particular hassle because there are so many. And what's the function of those mysterious punctuation marks–the semicolon, colon, dash, and apostrophe?

Editing punctuation can be an easy job if you approach it from the Big Picture. Instead of coming to every sentence as though it's unique, choosing a punctuation mark because "it sounds right," learn the Big Picture patterns that underlie *all* sentences. Once you learn Four Basic Sentence types, you can apply them to any possible sentence. No sentence is unique. You thus need to memorize the Four Basic Sentences.

Let's begin with the simple sentence. Most writers never have a problem punctuating the simple sentence when it requires just a *final* punctuation mark.

- ▶ **I drove Sandy to soccer practice.**
- ▶ **Will you drive Sandy to soccer practice?**
- ▶ **Please drive Sandy to soccer practice!**

The problem comes when we need–or think we need–something in the middle of the sentence, or what is called "internal punctuation."

> **WRONG: I drove Sandy, to soccer practice.**
> **WRONG: Will you please drive Sandy; to soccer practice?**
> **WRONG: Please drive Sandy to: soccer practice!**

Along with the apostrophe, internal punctuation causes most of our punctuation problems. Internal punctuation includes the comma, semicolon, colon, dash, parentheses, and brackets.

> And that long list probably looks like you have to learn a bunch of rules . . .
> But you don't.

The Trick to Mastering Punctuation

There's a trick to mastering punctuation, and especially basic comma rules. If you take all sentences that need internal punctuation and boil them down–reduce them to basic building blocks–you'll end up with just *four* basic sentence types.

So here's the trick: The easy way to master punctuation is to learn what punctuation all four require. If you do that, then you won't have to check the rules for every sentence you write. You'll know what to do because all sentences, other than the simple ones above, will *always* fall into one of these four types, no matter their infinite number of variations.

All four have a common denominator: *They have two parts* that variously combine the fragment and the sentence. Because all four sentences have two parts, they also share a second common denominator: *internal punctuation*, which is used to separate the two parts. You won't always need internal punctuation with the four sentence types, but when you do, to punctuate properly, you have to be able to tell a fragment from a sentence.

The Fragment

The fragment is a *fragment*–that is, a *part*–of a sentence. By definition, a fragment *doesn't make sense by itself*. To make sense, a <u>fragment</u> needs more information to complete it. That "more information" comes in a short sentence that's part of a bigger sentence, the one that ends with the final period.

Fragment + Short sentence = Bigger Sentence.

- **<u>Because Andrea was sick,</u> I stayed home.**
- **<u>If you come to our place tonight,</u> we will cook you dinner.**
- **<u>After Frank leaves the house,</u> his dog begins to bark.**

Note that, for each fragment, you can ask a "more information, please" question that the short sentence answers.

- **What happened because Andrea was sick? (I stayed home.)**

- **What will happen if you come to our place tonight? (We will cook you dinner.)**

- **What happens after Frank leaves the house? (His dog begins to bark.)**

Sometimes fragments are exactly what a writer needs, especially fiction writers who use the fragment for a special effect. But academic writers, who try to present their ideas free of distraction, avoid the fragment when it's not user-friendly. A fragment can distract the reader from the flow; he has to pause to figure things out. Look at the next example. Does the <u>fragment</u> belong to the sentence on the left or to the sentence on the right?

- **I tried to get off work. <u>Because I wanted to go to the concert.</u> I was upset that my boss said I couldn't leave.**

You can't tell. Writing teachers frown on fragments like this. The reader jerks to a stop. What is the writer trying to say? That ambiguity is one reason why academic writing avoids fragments.

The Dependent Clause

There are two kinds of fragments–the kind that has a <u>subject</u> and verb and the kind that doesn't. The kind that does is called a *dependent clause*. (It *depends* on more information to make sense; by itself, a dependent clause doesn't make sense because it's a fragment of a complete thought, that is, of a sentence.)

Fragments with a <u>Subject</u> and Verb = Dependent Clauses

- ► **because <u>Andrea</u> was sick (what? more information, please)**
- ► **if <u>you</u> come to our place tonight (what? more information, please)**
- ► **after <u>Frank</u> leaves the house (what? more information, please)**

The Phrase

The kind of fragment that doesn't have a subject and verb is called a *phrase*. A prepositional phrase is one example of a phrase. (Prepositions are those little words that glue sentence parts together: *in*, *at*, *for*, *by*, *up*, *down*, *with*, *through*, *over*, *out*, etc.). Other kinds of phrases include the infinitive phrase and the participial phrase.

Fragments without a Subject and Verb = Phrases

- ► **in the first fifty days**
- ► **at the last hearing**
- ► **for each woman**

By itself, like the dependent clause, the phrase doesn't make sense. And like the dependent clause, the phrase is a <u>fragment</u>–a fragment of a sentence. To make sense, a phrase needs more information to complete the thought. (Again, that "more information" comes in a short sentence that's part of a bigger sentence, the one that ends with the final period.)

<u>Fragment</u> + Short sentence = Bigger Sentence.

- ► <u>**In the first fifty days**</u>**, the new administration accomplished a great deal.**
- ► <u>**At the last hearing,**</u> **our witness testified quite effectively.**
- ► <u>**For each woman,**</u> **beating her team's archrival was more than just a victory.**

The Sentence (The Independent Clause)

Like a dependent clause, an independent clause has both a <u>subject</u> and verb. But unlike the dependent clause and the phrase, the independent clause *makes sense by itself*. It doesn't need more words to complete the thought. That's why it's called an *independent clause*. (Independently, by itself, the sentence offers a complete thought. It doesn't depend on other words because it stands on its own.)

Sentences = Independent Clauses.

- ► **Because Andrea was sick, <u>I</u> stayed home.**
- ► **If you come to our place tonight, <u>we</u> will cook you dinner.**
- ► **After Frank leaves the house, his <u>dog</u> begins to bark.**

> **PUNCTUATION TIP**
> Sentences belong to a context. Every sentence must
> somehow connect to the sentence it follows and the
> sentence it precedes; all together, those sentences belong to
> a bigger context, which may be the argument you're making
> in a paragraph. Nevertheless, if you pull a sentence out of its
> context, no matter how obscure or odd it may sound, it's still
> a sentence because it's a complete thought.

To test whether you have a fragment or a sentence, read the words out loud. The sentence doesn't automatically require more words to complete it. It's independent. But the fragment does–because it's a fragment of a thought. Now read the following sentences and fragments out loud.

- ▶ **Go down to the cellar.** (*sentence = complete thought*)
- ▶ **before you go down to the cellar** (*dependent clause fragment = incomplete thought*)
- ▶ **Nobody knew anything.** (*sentence = complete thought*)
- ▶ **because nobody knew anything** (*dependent clause fragment = incomplete thought*)
- ▶ **In the beginning, the seas enveloped the planet.** (*sentence = complete thought*)
- ▶ **in the beginning** (*phrase fragment = incomplete thought*)

This test isn't foolproof, but if you read a sentence out loud, it tends to sound finished, complete, whereas a fragment sounds unfinished, left hanging: *Before you go down to the cellar–(?)*

The Four Basic Sentences

Each of the four basic sentence types has two parts. Three of the four combine a fragment (F) and a sentence (S). The fourth combines a sentence (S) and a sentence (S).

The fragment can be either a dependent clause ("because Andrea was sick") or a phrase ("in the first fifty days").

1. **Basic Sentence FS = a fragment** *plus* **a sentence** (= *a bigger sentence*)
2. **Basic Sentence SF = a sentence** *plus* **a fragment** (= *a bigger sentence*)
3. **Basic Sentence $\overuparrow{SFS}$ = a fragment** *inside* **a sentence** (= *a bigger sentence*)
4. **Basic Sentence SS = a sentence** *plus* **another sentence** (= *a bigger sentence*)

(The loop above the third type, $\overuparrow{SFS}$, indicates that you have one sentence cut in half, not two sentences; only the fourth type, SS, has two sentences.)

These four sentences break into eight patterns. Each pattern is punctuated differently.

1. Basic Sentence FS Pattern 1 (F,S)	*2. Basic Sentence SF* Pattern 2 (SF) Pattern 3 (S,F)
3. Basic Sentence S͡FS͡ Pattern 4 (S͡FS͡) Pattern 5 (S͡,F,S͡)	*4. Basic Sentence SS* Pattern 6 (S, conj S) Pattern 7 (S./; S) Pattern 8 (S./; trans, S)

1. Basic Sentence FS

Pattern 1 (F,S)

After <u>an introductory fragment</u>, use the comma.

- ► **Because Andrea was sick, I stayed home.** (*fragment = dependent clause*)
- ► **In the first fifty days, the new administration accomplished a great deal.** (*fragment = phrase*)

> **PUNCTUATION TIP**
> When the introductory fragment is no more than three or four short words, some writers and publications leave out the comma. This is a matter of style and preference. To be safe (and correct), you can always use the comma. Using the comma will give your writing clarity and consistency.

2. Basic Sentence SF

Pattern 2 (SF)

Don't use the comma before an <u>essential fragment</u>. ("Essential" means that you *can't* get rid of the fragment. It's needed to provide essential information about the rest of the sentence. Without that information, the reader is left hanging: *Why?*)

- ► **I had to book my hotel online <u>because I was trying to save money</u>.** (***Why*** **did you have to book your hotel online? The essential fragment gives the reason.** *fragment = dependent clause*)
- ► **I had to book my hotel online <u>to save money</u>.** (***Why*** **did you have to book your hotel online? The essential fragment gives the reason.** *fragment = infinitive phrase*)

Pattern 3 (S,F)

*Use the comma before a **nonessential fragment**.* ("Nonessential" means that you *can* get rid of the fragment. It provides nonessential information about the rest of the sentence.)

▶ **I called my brother, <u>although I had a lot to do at work</u>. (The sentence doesn't need nonessential information provided by the fragment. The information is perhaps interesting but in no way essential to explain *why* you called your brother. *fragment = dependent clause*)**

▶ **I called my brother. (The sentence is a complete thought that doesn't require more information to complete it.)**

▶ **I called my brother, <u>with real regret</u>. (*fragment = prepositional phrase*)**

▶ **I called my brother, <u>to speak of real regret</u>. (*fragment = infinitive phrase*)**

▶ **I called my brother, <u>having real regret</u>. (*fragment = participial phrase*)**

▶ **I called my brother. (The sentence doesn't need nonessential information provided by the fragments.)**

It helps to know the words that start essential and nonessential fragments. Some words start only essential fragments, and some start only nonessential, but some can start both (depending on context).

ESSENTIAL	NONESSENTIAL	BOTH
as . . . as	all of which	after
for	although	as
so . . . that	even though	as if
than	no matter how/what/why	as though
that	none of which/whom	at/by/for/in which
until	some of which/whom	because
	whereas	before
	which	if
		in order that
		unless
		what
		when
		where
		while
		who
		whom
		whose

ALWAYS ESSENTIAL: The girl danced as dramatically as she always had.

ALWAYS NONESSENTIAL: The noisy Cub Scouts sang loudly, which annoyed their scoutmaster.

BOTH: I saw the man who was training for the Olympics. (essential) I saw Kenyon, who was training for the Olympics. (nonessential)

3. Basic Sentence S͡FS

Pattern 4 (S͡FS)

Don't use commas for an <u>*essential fragment*</u> *inside a* <u>*sentence.*</u> (The fragment identifies the subject and thus is essential.)

▶ **The man <u>who sells fish</u> also sells aquariums.**
(The essential fragment identifies *which* man also sells aquariums–the man <u>who sells fish</u>. Leaving out the fragment will cause confusion: *Which* man do you mean? *fragment = dependent clause*)

▶ **The woman <u>wearing the red shirt</u> also sells aquariums.**
(The essential fragment identifies *which* woman also sells aquariums–the woman <u>wearing the red shirt</u>. Leaving out the fragment will cause confusion: *Which* woman do you mean? *fragment = participial phrase*)

▶ **My brother <u>Bob</u> also sells aquariums.**
(The essential fragment identifies *which* brother also sells aquariums. Here we can assume you have more than one brother and need the fragment to distinguish your brother Bob from your brother Tom and your brother Bill. Leaving out the necessary fragment will cause confusion: *Which* brother do you mean? *fragment = appositive, a word or phrase renaming a noun*)

Pattern 5 (S͡,F,S)

Use commas for a <u>*nonessential fragment*</u> *inside a* <u>*sentence.*</u> (The fragment isn't needed since the subject is already identified.)

▶ **Mr. Mason, <u>who sells fish</u>, also sells aquariums.**
(The nonessential fragment isn't needed to identify the subject. He's already identified by name: Mr. Mason. Leaving out the fragment won't cause confusion. *fragment = dependent clause*)

▶ **Frieda Wilson, <u>wearing the red shirt</u>, also sells aquariums.**
(The nonessential fragment isn't needed to identify the subject. She's already identified by name: Frieda Wilson. Leaving out the fragment won't cause confusion. *fragment = participial phrase*)

▶ **My brother, <u>Bob</u>, also sells aquariums.**
(The nonessential fragment isn't needed to identify the subject. Here we will assume you have only one brother. The fragment isn't needed to distinguish one brother from another since you have only one. *fragment = appositive*)

► **My brother, <u>however,</u> also sells aquariums.**
► **My brother, <u>on the other hand,</u> also sells aquariums.**
(The nonessential fragments interrupt the "flow" of each sentence. Like many interrupting transitions, *however* and *on the other hand* can be left out without causing confusion. *fragment = transition, a word or phrase used to connect one part to another*)

4. Basic Sentence SS

Pattern 6 (S, conj S)

Use the comma *BEFORE the* coordinating conjunctions *for, and, nor, but, or, yet, so (the FANBOYS) to separate two* <u>sentences.</u>

► <u>**I went to the store, for** I needed some bread.</u>
► <u>**Bob went to the store, and** he bought some bread.</u>
► <u>**The girl went to the store, yet** she forgot to buy some bread.</u>

Pattern 7 (S./;S)

Use the period *to separate two unrelated* <u>sentences;</u> *use the* period *or* semicolon *to separate two related* <u>sentences.</u>

► <u>Marilyn Monroe was a famous movie blonde "bombshell."</u>
  <u>George W. Bush moved to Texas.</u> (*unrelated sentences= period*)
► <u>Marilyn Monroe was a famous movie blonde "bombshell."</u>
  <u>Movies' first blonde bombshell was Jean Harlow.</u> (*related sentences = period or semicolon*)
► <u>Marilyn Monroe was a famous movie blonde "bombshell";</u>
  <u>movies' first blonde bombshell was Jean Harlow.</u> (*related sentences = period or semicolon*)

Pattern 8 (S./; trans, S)

Use the period **or** semicolon **to separate two related sentences linked with a transition; use the** comma **after the transition.***
  ***Excluding one-word transitions:** *hence, next, now, then, thus,* etc.

► <u>Marilyn Monroe was a famous movie blonde "bombshell."</u>
  <u>However, movies' first blonde bombshell was Jean Harlow.</u>
► <u>Marilyn Monroe was a famous movie blonde "bombshell";</u>
  <u>however, movies' first blonde bombshell was Jean Harlow.</u>

The period and the semicolon have the same function–to separate sentences. Writers choose the semicolon over the period when they want to emphasize the relation that one sentence has with another.

The Apostrophe '

The apostrophe has three uses:

1. To show possession
2. To replace letters
3. To form nonstandard plurals

> **PUNCTUATION TIP**
> No other punctuation mark faces so much abuse as the apostrophe. The first problem is failing to use it (thus we see *Walgreens* instead of *Walgreen's*). The second problem is, ironically, using it in words where it doesn't belong (*Open Monday's*).

To show possession

1. **Use the apostrophe to show possession. To know where to place the apostrophe, say the word. Where the word stops, add the apostrophe: the cat–the cat's dish; the cats–the cats' dish.**

   Karl's book; both Karls' books (two men named Karl)
   everybody's response; someone else's car
   city's lights; cities' lights; baby's crib; babies' cribs
   the man's hat; the men's hats
   the woman's computer; the women's computer
   bachelor's degree; master's degree
   Paul Smith's house; the Smiths' house
   Katie said, "Aren't they at the Smiths'?"
   Roger and Bill's book (the one book belongs to both Roger and Bill)
   Roger's and Bill's books (each owns a book)
   Jean-Luc's singing is enjoyable, and so is Linda's whistling
       (possessive apostrophe needed for the gerund: a noun that comes
       from a verb and ends in *-ing*)
   the hostess's party; the hostesses' parties
   Mrs. Phillips's cell phone

If adding an extra syllable makes the word hard to pronounce, add only the apostrophe.

   Mrs. Phillips' cell phone
   Athens' famous sights
   for goodness' sake

> **WARNING**
>
> **Don't use the apostrophe with seven possessive pronouns:** *yours, his, hers, ours, theirs, its* (**versus the contraction** *it's = it is* **or** *it has*)**, and** *whose* (**versus the contraction** *who's = who is* **or** *who has*).

This book is yours; the car is his or hers; the job is ours; the job is theirs. Its color is green. (It's raining outside; it's been raining all afternoon.) Whose responsibility is this? (Who's going to volunteer? Who's volunteered before?)

To replace letters

2. **Use the apostrophe to replace letters.**

    it's = it is or it has
    shouldn't = should not
    they're = they are
    the class of '91 = the class of 1991
    'til = until
    Hallowe'en = Halloween

To form nonstandard plurals

3. **Use the apostrophe to form nonstandard plurals: for letters, numbers used as words, words cited as words, abbreviations, and symbols.**

    CAPITAL LETTERS: Watch your P's and Q's. A's win the pennant.

    LOWERCASE LETTERS: Watch your p's and q's.

    NUMBERS USED AS WORDS: He crosses his 7's. (= sevens) He often talks about the 1980's. (= nineteen eighties)

    WORDS CITED AS WORDS: Please practice pronouncing your the's.

    ABBREVIATIONS: The professors all have Ph.D.'s.

    SYMBOLS: I saw +'s and -'s in the grade book.

For this third use, leave out the apostrophe if there's no danger of confusion:

    Watch your Ps and Qs.
    He crosses his 7s.
    He talks often about the 1980s.
    The professors all have Ph.D.s.
    can'ts, don'ts, won'ts
    ifs, ands, or buts; ins and outs

But with confusion, use the apostrophe:

> As win the pennant! (confusion with *As*)
> A's win the pennant.

> Watch your ps and qs. (confusion with a misprint)
> Watch your p's and q's.

> Please practice pronouncing your thes. (confusion with a misprint)
> Please practice pronouncing your the's.

> I saw +s and -s in the grade book (confusion if symbols unclear)
> I saw +'s and -'s in the grade book.

WARNING

Remember that most words don't use the apostrophe to form plurals.

WRONG	RIGHT
mens shoe's	men's shoes
open Sunday's	open Sundays
seven month's of the year	seven months of the year

Brackets [ ]

Brackets have two uses:

1. **To show an insertion within parentheses**
2. **To show an editor's insertion into a text**

To show an insertion within parentheses

1. **Use brackets to show "parentheses" within parentheses.**

   My friend George Washington (who is not *that* George Washington [the Father of Our Country]) often gets teased about his famous name.

To show an editor's insertion into a text

1. **Use brackets to show that you as editor are supplying missing words or identifying a mistake in the original text.**
   He wrote, "I'll see you at Tom's [cabin]."
   (To clarify, the editor supplies a missing word.)

   "The defendant [Lloyd Turner] was charged with a felony (though later acquitted)."
   (The editor uses brackets and not parentheses for new insertions. In the original text, the writer showed his insertion with parentheses; in the edited text, the editor shows her new insertion with brackets.)

"We reached our destanation [*sic*] after many wrong detours."
(By using the Latin word *sic*, the editor identifies a mistake in the original text–"destanation" should be spelled "destination." The Latin *sic* means *thus*: *Thus it was written in the original and is not the editor's mistake.* In this case, the editor chooses not to correct the mistake but to signal to the reader that the original text erred.)

"World War II ended in 1947 [*sic*]."
(The editor identifies the writer's mistake: World War II ended in 1945, not 1947.)

The Colon :

The colon has two uses:

1. **To set up material**
2. **To separate a bigger part from a smaller part**

To set up material

1. **Use the colon to set up a list within a sentence.**

   I visited four cities: Omaha, Denver, Salt Lake City, and Dallas.

2. **Use the colon to set up a list in a column.**

   The company needs to focus on four Asian markets:
   China
   Japan
   South Korea
   Thailand

3. **Use the colon to set up an important idea.**

   Martin Luther King, Jr., changed the face of America: He spearheaded the modern Civil Rights movement.
   Beatriz has a single joy in life: music.

PUNCTUATION TIP
Writers tend to forget the colon. Like the semicolon, the colon gives writing efficiency and professionalism.
For example, it can serve as a space-saving transition to set up an important idea (see **Colon 3**, above). Here, replacing *therefore* with the colon saves a word.

> **WITH TRANSITION WORD:** *Teddy Roosevelt was a keen environmentalist. Therefore, he worked hard to establish a system of national parks.*
> **WITH COLON:** *Teddy Roosevelt was a keen environmentalist: He worked hard to establish a system of national parks.*

4. **Use the colon to set up a well-known or long quotation.**

   Hamlet said: "To be or not to be."

   > **PUNCTUATION TIP**
   > The comma can also work in the previous sentence, but the colon establishes the fame or seriousness of the quotation.

5. Use the colon to set up a quotation not introduced by a verb (*said*, *declared*, *stated*, etc.).

   Many Americans recall a line from John F. Kennedy's most famous speech: "And so, my fellow Americans, ask not what your country can do for you; ask what you can do for your country."

6. **Use the colon to start (to set up) a formal letter.**

   Dear Dr. Smith:
   Ladies and Gentlemen:

7. **Use the colon to punctuate setup headers in memos.**

   To:
   From:
   Re:

To separate a bigger part from a smaller part

8. **Use the colon in time references, scriptural references, citation references, and subtitles.**

   3:47 p.m. (separating hour from minute)

   Leviticus 7:14 (separating Bible chapter from verse)

   "Revisiting the Museum: Picasso and the Art of the Unknown." *Art Journal* 121.1 (2007): 132-56. Print. (separating citation from page)

   Pip's Journey from Snobbery to Salvation: Magwitch and the Lessons of Love in *Great Expectations* (separating title from subtitle)

   > **WARNING**
   >
   > **Be careful with the colon in the next FOUR situations..**

1. **Do not use the colon AFTER *such as* and *like*.**

   WRONG: He listened to many classical composers, such as: Bach and Brahms.
   RIGHT: He listened to many classical composers, such as Bach and Brahms.

WRONG: He listened to many classical composers, like: Bach and Brahms.
RIGHT: He listened to many classical composers, like Bach and Brahms.

2. **Ordinarily, do not use the colon AFTER a <u>verb of being</u> (*am, are, is, were, was, will be*, etc.) or AFTER a <u>preposition</u> (*in, of, by, at*, etc.).**

   WRONG: His favorite foods <u>are:</u> steak and potatoes
   RIGHT: His favorite foods are steak and potatoes.

   WRONG: I want to major <u>in:</u> music and history.
   RIGHT: I want to major in music and history.

   WRONG: The recipe primarily consisted <u>of:</u> zucchini and Indian spices.
   RIGHT: The recipe primarily consisted of zucchini and Indian spices.

   WRONG: The book is <u>by:</u> James McKinley, and it's available <u>at:</u> the bookstore.
   RIGHT: The book is by James McKinley, and it's available at the bookstore.

3. **Do not use the colon INSIDE quotation marks and parentheses.**

   WRONG: Here's why you should read Hemingway's "Soldier's Home:" It dramatizes the pressures that cause us to conform.
   RIGHT: Here's why you should read Hemingway's "Soldier's Home": It dramatizes the pressures that cause us to conform.
   WRONG: Here's why you should read Hemingway's best story ("Soldier's Home":) It dramatizes the pressures that cause us to conform.
   RIGHT: Here's why you should read Hemingway's best story ("Soldier's Home"): It dramatizes the pressures that cause us to conform.

4. **Capitalize AFTER a colon if a <u>complete sentence</u> follows. Don't capitalize if a <u>fragment</u> follows.**

   COMPLETE SENTENCE: Here's why you should read Hemingway's "Soldier's Home": <u>It dramatizes the pressures that cause us to conform.</u>
   FRAGMENT: Here's what you'll find in Hemingway's "Soldier's Home": a masterly dramatization of the pressures that cause us to conform.

The Comma **,**

The comma has three uses:

1. **To separate a fragment from the main part of a sentence**
2. **To separate equal sentences or equal sentence parts**
3. **To replace words**

PUNCTUATION TIP
In order, the three most common comma errors are
(1) forgetting to use the comma AFTER an introductory
fragment, (2) forgetting to use the comma BEFORE a
coordinating conjunction to separate two complete
sentences, and (3) mistakenly putting a comma between
two complete sentences and thus creating a run-on (see
Semicolon 1, page 107).

To separate a fragment from the main part of a sentence

1. **Use the comma AFTER an** <u>introductory fragment</u> **to separate it from the main part of a sentence.**

   WRONG: <u>Yes</u> I have many concerns about the merger.
   RIGHT: <u>Yes,</u> I have many concerns about the merger.
   WRONG: <u>After the party fizzled out</u> we walked home.
   RIGHT: <u>After the party fizzed out,</u> we walked home.

2. **Use the comma for a** nonessential interrupting fragment **to separate it from the main part of a sentence. (An "interrupting fragment" is a fragment inserted into the middle of a sentence. See the following for a discussion of "nonessential" and "essential.")**

Nonessential interrupter

   SENTENCE: My father became a Marine.
   INTERRUPTING FRAGMENT: who is older than his sister
   SENTENCE WITH INTERRUPTING FRAGMENT: My father who is older than his sister became a Marine.
   NONESSENTIAL OR ESSENTIAL? If it's nonessential, use commas; if it's essential, don't use commas.
   TEST FOR COMMAS: Can you identify the <u>subject</u> (who the father is) by leaving out the interrupting fragment?
   ANSWER: Yes. The interrupting fragment offers interesting information, but it's not essential to identifying the subject since we have "my" and only one father.
   RULE: If you *don't* need the interrupting fragment to identify the subject, it's nonessential. Thus use commas.
   THUS: My father, who is older than his sister, became a Marine.

My <u>father, Tom,</u> became a Marine.

(Into *My father became a Marine* insert the interrupting fragment that renames the <u>subject</u>. Since we know it's "*my* father," the fragment is nonessential. Use commas for this nonessential called an "appositive." See **Comma 8**, page 100.)

My brother, likewise, became a Marine.

(Into *My brother became a Marine* insert the interrupting fragment *likewise*; because it's nonessential, use commas.)

My daily schedule, if all goes well, will include an hour at the gym.

(Into *My daily schedule will include an hour at the gym* insert the interrupting fragment *if all goes well*; because it's nonessential, use commas.)

All through the night, because of financial worries, I kept waking up.

(Into *All through the night, I kept waking up* insert the interrupting fragment *because of financial worries*; because it's nonessential, use commas.)

Essential interrupting fragment

SENTENCE: The man is tall.
INTERRUPTING FRAGMENT: who called me last night
SENTENCE WITH INTERRUPTING FRAGMENT: The man who called me last night is tall.
ESSENTIAL OR NONESSENTIAL? If it's essential, don't use commas; if it's nonessential, use commas.
TEST FOR COMMAS: Can you identify the <u>subject</u> (which man you're talking about) by leaving out the interrupting fragment? ***The man is tall.***
ANSWER: No. "The man" doesn't identify *which* man is tall. Many men are tall. You need the interrupting fragment **who called me last night** to distinguish this man from all other men.
RULE: If you *need* the interrupting fragment to identify the subject, it's essential. Thus don't use commas.
THUS: The man who called me last night is tall.

3. **Use the comma to separate a nonessential final fragment from the main part of a sentence.**

I saw my brother <u>Tom, who became a Marine.</u>

(Since the direct object, <u>Tom,</u> is identified, the final fragment is nonessential and requires a comma. Compare to *I saw my brother who became a Marine*. With just one brother, the fragment isn't needed. *I saw my brother, who became a Marine*. With more than one brother, the fragment is needed to distinguish *this* brother from other brothers–and thus the comma isn't used: *I saw my brother who became a Marine*.)

4. **Use the comma to separate a nonessential fragment introduced by *which* from the main part of a sentence.**

The attic front <u>window</u>, which I must replace, was broken in the hail storm.
(Just one attic front window = *which*.)

The <u>White House</u>, which I visited last year, opens its doors to tourists.
(Just one White House = *which*.)

The <u>Pacific Ocean</u>, which the sailor crossed on a raft, is full of treacherous currents.
(Just one Pacific Ocean = *which*.)

WARNING

When you have more than one of something, use *that* without a comma to introduce an essential fragment–a fragment identifying the <u>subject</u> and equal in importance to the main part of the sentence.

The <u>window</u> that was broken in the storm needs to be replaced.
(*Which* window? One of many–the one that was broken in the storm.)

The <u>house</u> that I visited last year opens its doors to tourists.
(*Which* house? One of many–the one that I visited last year.)

The <u>ocean</u> that the sailor crossed on a raft is full of treacherous currents.
(*Which* ocean? One of many–the one that the sailor crossed on a raft.)

To separate equal sentences or equal sentence parts

5. **Use the comma BEFORE the coordinating conjunctions *for*, *<u>a</u>nd*, *<u>n</u>or*, *<u>b</u>ut*, *<u>o</u>r*, *<u>y</u>et*, *<u>s</u>o* (the FANBOYS) to separate <u>equal sentences</u>. (They're equal because they're both complete sentences, or independent clauses.)**

<u>I prepared my taxes in a hurry</u>, for <u>tomorrow was the April 15 deadline</u>.
<u>I prepared my taxes in a hurry</u>, and <u>I had done the same thing the year before</u>.
<u>I prepared my taxes</u>, but <u>I put the task off until the last day</u>.
<u>I prepared my taxes in a hurry</u>, so <u>I hoped that I hadn't made a mistake</u>.

6. **Use the comma to separate *three* or more equal items in a <u>series</u>; last comma = optional.**

   George Clooney is <u>tall, dark(,) and handsome</u>.

7. Use the comma to separate <u>adjectives</u> that equally describe the same noun.

   I saw the <u>tired, old</u> man.
   (I saw the <u>old, tired</u> man.)

   PUNCTUATION TIP
   To test for the comma, try inverting the adjectives. If you can't invert them, they're not equal. Don't use the comma.

   > I saw the <u>old stone</u> fence.

   (The inversion, "<u>stone old</u>," makes no sense because "old" and "stone" don't equally describe "fence.")

   ---

8. **Use the comma to separate an <u>appositive</u> from the noun it renames. (An "appositive" is a word or phrase renaming a *one-of-a-kind* noun that it follows. The appositive is equal to the noun and is a "nonessential interrupting fragment." See Comma 2, page 97.)**

   My wife, <u>Carol,</u> tracks the flight of whooping cranes.
   (Since you have just *one* wife, she is a *one-of-a-kind* noun. Use commas to set off the appositive that renames it, Carol.)

   My brother, <u>Tom,</u> joined the Marines.
   (If you have just *one* brother, use commas. For more than one brother, don't use commas: *My brother Tom joined the Marines, but my brother Joe joined the Air Force.*)

   Jimmy Carter, <u>one of our ex-Presidents,</u> has written a novel.
   (Since there is just one Jimmy Carter who is an ex-President, use commas.)

9. **Use the comma to separate a final <u>question</u> from the rest of a sentence.**

   It's supposed to rain, <u>isn't it?</u>
   (The question serves as a balancing equal to the first part of the sentence.)
   You're not really going, <u>are you?</u>

10. **Use the comma to separate <u>balanced, equal phrases</u>.**

    <u>The less</u> I know, <u>the better</u>.
    <u>garbage in</u>, <u>garbage out</u>
    <u>the more</u>, <u>the merrier</u>
    <u>first come</u>, <u>first served</u>
    I like <u>his politics</u>, not <u>his personality</u>.

11. **Use the comma to separate equal items in dates, addresses, geographical sites, and numbers.**

    WRONG: September 11, 2001 is an important date.
    RIGHT: September 11, 2001, is an important date.
    BUT: I will contact him in June 2012 in Chicago. (Don't use the comma with just month and year.)

    WRONG: He lives at 3925 East Johnson, Madison, Wisconsin, 53704. (Never separate state from zip code with the comma.)
    RIGHT: He lives at 3925 East Johnson, Madison, Wisconsin 53704.

    WRONG: I drove to New York, New York and then flew to London, England before taking the train to Paris.
    RIGHT: I drove to New York, New York, and then flew to London, England, before taking the train to Paris.

    WRONG: Please make sure that 6000545 is the correct population.
    RIGHT: Please make sure that 6,000,545 is the correct population.

To replace words

12. **Use the comma to replace <u>words left out</u> of the second half of a parallel sentence.**

    He likes comedies; his wife, dramas.
    　　(He likes comedies; his wife <u>likes</u> dramas.)

    Americans prefer football; Europeans, soccer.
    　　(Americans prefer football; Europeans <u>prefer</u> soccer.)

13. **Use the comma to replace *that*.**

    The problem is, Bob can't sing tonight.
    　　(The problem is that Bob can't sing tonight.)

    Odds are, you won't pass the course if you don't study.
    　　(Odds are that you won't pass the course if you don't study.)

> **WARNING**
>
> **Avoid the following TEN comma errors.**

1. **Don't use the comma (or nothing at all) between <u>two complete sentences</u>; you'll cause a run-on.***
   WRONG: <u>I drove to work, I parked my car in the underground garage</u>.
   (**WRONG:** <u>I drove to work I parked my car in the underground garage</u>.)
   RIGHT: I drove to work. I parked my car in the underground garage.
   RIGHT: I drove to work; I parked my car in the underground garage.
   RIGHT: I drove to work, and I parked my car in the underground garage.

PUNCTUATION TIP

A *run-on* is defined by faulty punctuation, not by the length of the sentence. Two problems cause the run-on: (1) Putting a comma between two complete sentences instead of a period, semicolon, or comma plus conjunction. (2) Leaving out *all* punctuation between two complete sentences.

---

2. **Don't use the comma BEFORE a <u>coordinating conjunction</u> if a fragment follows the conjunction.**

   WRONG: Nedra bought groceries, <u>and</u> then gas.
   RIGHT: Nedra bought groceries and then gas.
   WRONG: The girl plays the piano, <u>and</u> sings in the choir.
   RIGHT: The girl plays piano and sings in the choir.
   (**BUT:** The girl plays the piano, <u>and</u> she sings in the choir. See **Comma 5**, page 99.)

3. **Don't use the comma AFTER a <u>coordinating conjunction</u> in sentences like the following.**

   WRONG: <u>But,</u> I think you're wrong about the movie.
   RIGHT: But I think you're wrong about the movie.
   WRONG: <u>And,</u> that's just the beginning of the story.
   RIGHT: And that's just the beginning of the story.

4. **Don't use the comma AFTER *though*, *although*, and *even though* in sentences like the following.**

   WRONG: Though, your plan has merit, please refigure the budget.
   RIGHT: Though your plan has merit, please refigure the budget.

WRONG: Brian plans to open a restaurant although, many say he won't succeed.
RIGHT: Brian plans to open a restaurant although many say he won't succeed.

5. **Don't use the comma AFTER *such as*, *especially*, or *also* in sentences like the following.**

    WRONG: He visited many famous parks, such as, Yosemite and Glacier.
    RIGHT: He visited many famous parks, such as Yosemite and Glacier.
    WRONG: He liked to visit famous parks, especially, Yosemite and Glacier.
    RIGHT: He liked to visit famous parks, especially Yosemite and Glacier.
    WRONG: He also, liked to visit famous landmarks.
    RIGHT: He also liked to visit famous landmarks.

6. **Don't use the comma to separate a <u>subject</u> from its verb. This error often happens when a verb (like *is* or *was*) comes late in a sentence.**

    WRONG: <u>Everything</u> that the restaurant serves every day of the week, is vegetarian.
    RIGHT: Everything that the restaurant serves every day of the week is vegetarian.
    WRONG: The autographed <u>baseball</u> that my uncle gave me for my birthday, arrived in the mail.
    RIGHT: The autographed baseball that my uncle gave me for my birthday arrived in the mail.

7. **Don't use the comma to separate a <u>verb</u> from its direct object. This error often happens BEFORE *that* or other clause words like *how*.**

    WRONG: John <u>told</u> the group, that he wanted to reorganize our bylaws.
    RIGHT: John told the group that he wanted to reorganize our bylaws.
    WRONG: I never appreciated from my patients' eyes, how much they suffered.
    RIGHT: I never appreciated from my patients' eyes how much they suffered.

8. **Don't use the comma to separate the <u>main part of a sentence</u> from a final fragment that *completes* the main part of the sentence. (Final fragments often start with clause words like *because, since, though, although, even though, while, despite, in spite of, if, as, before, after, that*, and *how*. Final fragments that**

complete the main part are essential; those that don't, nonessential.)

WRONG: <u>Cynthia hoped to enter college,</u> because she wanted to get a pharmacy degree.

> (*Why* did Cynthia hope to enter college? You need *because she wanted to get a pharmacy degree* to complete the sentence by explaining *why*. The *because* is thus *essential*.)

RIGHT: Cynthia hoped to enter college because she wanted to get a pharmacy degree.

WRONG: <u>Sidney wanted to study the violin,</u> although she had no musical talent.

> (Sidney's lack of musical talent provides a necessary context for her desire to study the violin. The essential final fragment completes the sentence.)

RIGHT: Sidney wanted to study the violin although she had no musical talent.

9. **Don't use the comma to separate many internal transitions from the rest of the sentence.**

WRONG: I, also, must disagree with that.
RIGHT: I also must disagree with that. (**But:** Also, I must disagree with that.)
WRONG: I, nevertheless, disagree with that.
RIGHT: I nevertheless disagree with that. (**But:** Nevertheless, I disagree with that.)

WARNING

"Right" and "wrong" are not absolutes in this last rule. In general, the shorter the subject (*I, he, she, Bob, Jane*) and the shorter the transition (*too, also, in fact*), the less likely the comma will be needed. The longer the <u>subject</u> and transition and the greater the emphasis, the more likely you may wish to use it: <u>*President Franklin D. Roosevelt*</u>, *in the same manner, was able to overcome the psychologically crippling effects of polio.*

---

10. **Don't use the comma to separate an intensive pronoun from the rest of the sentence.**

WRONG: I, myself, will take care of planning the party.
RIGHT: I myself will take care of planning the party.
WRONG: Mrs. Steinberg wanted to speak with the supervisors, themselves.
RIGHT: Mrs. Steinberg wanted to speak with the supervisors themselves.
WRONG: The President, himself, will speak to the press.
RIGHT: The President himself will speak to the press.

Italics (Underlining) *italics* (underlining)

Italics have one use: *to set off special words*

NOTE: Italics = underlining (Underline if you're writing in longhand.)

1. **Use italics to set off these titles.**

Whole publications that have parts (chapters, articles, columns, features, etc.): books, newspapers, magazines, pamphlets

Each day she reads *The San Francisco Chronicle*.
(Each day she reads the San Francisco Chronicle.)
I subscribe to *The New Yorker*.
(I subscribe to The New Yorker.)

Long works of art that have parts (chapters, acts, episodes, movements, etc.): novels, long plays, long poems, movies, videos, TV and radio shows, ballets, musicals, operas, long musical works with descriptive titles

I read the novel *War and Peace*.
Do you know Carl Nielsen's Symphony No. 4, the *Inextinguishable*?

Paintings, drawings, prints, art installations, sculpture, and performance art

Vermeer's painting *Woman in Blue Reading a Letter*
Michelangelo's statue *David*
I saw Laurie Anderson perform her *Duets on Ice*.

Software and Web sites (but not individual Web pages)

WordPerfect still has its fans among desktop publishers.
The Internet Movie Database is my favorite Web site.

Records, DVDs, CDs, and video games

Music of Vienna offers a hundred-year-old boys' choir.

Ships, trains, and airplanes

Our train was the famous *City of San Francisco*.

WARNING

Don't put a comma BEFORE a title unless you're referring to a *one-of-a-kind* item.

WRONG: I read Hemingway's novel, *The Sun Also Rises.*
(The comma suggests that Hemingway wrote just one novel; since he published seven, the comma should be removed.)
RIGHT: I read Hemingway's novel *The Sun Also Rises.*
RIGHT: I read Salinger's novel, *The Catcher in the Rye.*
(Since Salinger published just one novel, the comma is correct.)

---

2. **Use italics or quotation marks to set off a special letter or word.**

The *e* in *mute* is silent.
We often use the word *really*. (We often use the word really.)
We often use the word "really."

3. **Use italics to set off foreign words not used in English.**

C'est pas vrai.
Lo siento mucho.
Dein blaues Auge

But don't use italics to set off foreign words that English has adopted.

aide-de-camp
enchilada
angst

Parentheses ( )

Parentheses have one use: *to show an insertion into a sentence*

1. **Use parentheses to show a parenthetical insertion (that is, material that offers information about the main sentence).**

The snow blanketed the driveway (a blizzard had blown in over the night), but we managed to back the car out.
The Academic Advancement Program (AAP) employs many deans.
John F. Kennedy (the thirty-fifth President of the United States) died in 1963.

PUNCTUATION TIP
When a parenthetically enclosed sentence stands completely separate from another sentence, start the enclosed sentence with a capital letter and place the period INSIDE the final parenthesis.

The snow blanketed the driveway. (A blizzard had blown in over the night.)

The Semicolon ;

The semicolon has two uses:

1. **To substitute for the period to separate related sentences**
2. **To separate items that have internal punctuation**

To substitute for the period to separate related sentences

1. Use the semicolon (and not the comma) to separate related sentences.

    I saw a famous French movie; it's called *La grande illusion.*
    Be sure to check the stove; I think I left the burner on.
    My daughter lives in Madison; my son lives in San Diego.

> **WARNING**
>
> **In the previous three sentences, using the comma instead of the semicolon will cause run-ons.**

2. **Use the semicolon to separate related sentences linked with a transition.**

    Eric stayed in Barcelona for a year; consequently, his Spanish improved considerably.
    Frank Sinatra was a good actor; however, it is as a singer that he is better known.

To separate items that have internal punctuation

3. **Use the semicolon to separate series units that have internal punctuation.**

                                                    1   2

    WRONG: We went to New York, New York, Detroit, Michigan,

             3

    and Seattle, Washington.

    RIGHT: We went to New York, New York; Detroit, Michigan; and Seattle, Washington.
    (Each of the three units in the series has its own comma between city and state, that is, "internal punctuation." Replace the commas *between* units with semicolons to avoid confusion.)

1. **The semicolon goes OUTSIDE the quotation marks and parentheses.**

    WRONG: I heard a song called "Fugue for Tinhorns;" Frank Loesser wrote the words and music.
    RIGHT: I heard a song called "Fugue for Tinhorns"; Frank Loesser wrote the words and music.

WRONG: I heard a song by Frank Loesser (an American composer of Broadway shows;) it's called "Fugue for Tinhorns."
RIGHT: I heard a song by Frank Loesser (an American composer of Broadway shows); it's called "Fugue for Tinhorns."

2. **Don't capitalize the first word AFTER the semicolon unless it's a <u>proper noun</u>.**

   WRONG: I saw the man in downtown Detroit; He was a resident.
   RIGHT: I saw the man in downtown Detroit; he was a resident.
   RIGHT: I saw the man in downtown Detroit; <u>Bob</u> was a resident.

3. **Don't use the semicolon to set up a <u>list</u>, either within a sentence or for a column (use the colon or dash).**

   WRONG: I visited four cities; <u>Omaha, Denver, Salt Lake City, and Dallas.</u>
   RIGHT: I visited four cities: Omaha, Denver, Salt Lake City, and Dallas.
   RIGHT: I visited four cities—Omaha, Denver, Salt Lake City, and Dallas.

4. Don't use the semicolon AFTER an <u>introductory fragment</u> (use the comma).

   WRONG: <u>Although I was too busy to notice</u>; it was raining all day.
   RIGHT: Although I was too busy to notice, it was raining all day.

5. Don't use the semicolon BEFORE a <u>nonessential final fragment</u> (use the comma).

   WRONG: It was raining all day; <u>although I was too busy to notice</u>.
   RIGHT: It was raining all day, although I was too busy to notice.